It Takes More Than a Chef

It Takes More Than a Chef

Wave Kasprzak

Monticello, Wisconsin
www.209main.com

It Takes More Than A Chef
Recipes & Stories from The Dining Room at 209 Main

First edition, first printing
Text copyright © 2010 by Wave Kasprzak
Photo copyright © 2010 by Good Food, Good People, Inc.

All rights reserved. No part of this publication may be reproduced, stored in a retrieval system, or transmitted, in any form or by any means, electronic, mechanical, photocopying, recording, or otherwise, in whole or part (except by a reviewer, who may quote short passages in a review), without the prior written permission from the publisher and author.

Design by Minglewood Design, Monticello, WI
Photos by Jane Sybers, Doug Whittle, Wave Kasprzak, Angie McGuire, Julie Doody.
Food styled by Wave Kasprzak.

Published by Good Food, Good People, Inc.
209 N. Main
Monticello, WI 53570

Contact
www.209main.com
to order more copies

ISBN 978-0-9831278-0-2

Printed in the United States
10 9 8 7 6 5 4 3 2 1

Table of Contents

Introduction 1
How We Started 2
Appetizers, Soups & Salads 4-38
Mothers 20
Cooking Classes 28
Side Dishes 40-57
Our Staff 58
Sauces 60-87
Reduction Sauces 89-103
Our Kids 104
Go-Alongs 106-119
Jane and Her Wine 120
Main Entrées 122-151
Camo Night 152
Desserts 154-171
After a Busy Night 172
About the Author 174
Index 177

Acknowledgements

A big thanks to everyone who made this book possible. Our guests, whether new or long time loyals. My cooking class students, some who have become good friends. And especially to Terese for her patience with my lack of computer skills. My wife Jane also for her patience with my lack of computer skills and just letting me do my own thing. Janet for her help and expertise in this new and scary venture. Debbie for her hard work when it was crunch time. Our great staff for making this whole machine work. And of course Jimmy for giving me Wednesday nights off to work on the book… and golf.

Introduction

My name is Wave Kasprzak. I have no formal culinary training, but cooking has been my profession since I was sixteen years old, and I'm a bit older than that now. I consider myself kind of a blue collar chef. I don't have a cooking show (yet). I don't have a signature exclamation, like "Bam!" or "Bon appétit!" I still work the line every night next to my co-workers.

My wife Jane Sybers and I own The Dining Room at 209 Main in Monticello, Wisconsin. We are open only four nights a week so that we can have time for a life outside of work. We love to play golf and watch football. Jane is a triathlete, and I practice and teach martial arts.

I hope that as you browse this book you will enjoy the sense of fun, adventure and humor I've tried to convey. I feel that cooking should be a good time. Cooks should take risks, experiment. They should laugh, too.

I look at recipes as guidelines that are as strict or loose as you want them to be. I always tell my cooking students to veer from recipes. I say, if you want to use more or less of an ingredient, or a different ingredient altogether, go for it. As far as I'm concerned, there are very few absolutes in cooking.

This book contains mostly recipes, but it also offers a little look at the people who make the restaurant work – our mothers, my cooking students, the staff. There are many integral parts to a restaurant. Everyone really needs to come together to make it all work. Without a doubt, it takes more than a chef.

How We Started

Shortly after Jane and I moved to southern Wisconsin's Green County, Jane's mother, Ruth, also moved here. I blame her for the start of the restaurant. Ruth bought the building that houses the restaurant back in 1996. It had been a classic Wisconsin tavern, but was now closed. Ruth asked if we wanted to open a restaurant in it and we immediately said no. "Just come and look at the space" she said. Soon the wheels started turning in our heads and the ideas started to form. Ruth suggested we give it a year and if it didn't work out then we could get out of it. With some remodeling, carpet and quite a bit of painting (believe me there was quite a bit of painting), we were ready to go.

We had worked in management in other restaurants and knew that it would mean long, exhausting hours and the kind of single-minded focus that too often left the rest of life in its dust. So we decided to set the hours that would afford us a lifestyle outside of work. We love to golf in the summer and watch football in the fall and winter. We also have a bit of property that needs attention, as in lawn mowing. Oh, and we wanted to stay married. So we decided to be open four nights a week, and add a fifth if needed, which we didn't need to do. We aren't getting rich, but we are happy and are running a successful business.

Even though we have white linen tablecloths and fresh flowers on the tables, when it comes right down to it we really are a Mom and Pop joint. Jane's in the front of the house (that means the dining room in restaurant lingo) greeting guests and I'm in the back of the house (read: kitchen) slingin' hash; that is, cooking pork tenderloin, pecan-crusted mahi mahi, and actual salmon hash.

Life is good.

"Opening Night"
September 25, 1996
The Dining Room
at
209 Main
Autumn Menu

Appetizers, Soups & Salads

It seems to me that a fair amount of the time the appetizers on a restaurant menu outshine the entrées. Sometimes when my wife Jane and I go out for dinner we'll end up just ordering a few appetizers, and a soup or salad. This is also a great way to taste a variety of dishes.

The recipes in this chapter are all three – appetizers, soups and salads. I feel that all can be great first courses to a meal, or make a meal themselves. For example, instead of having a sit-down dinner party, host a kind of mingling cocktail party, and serve a number of smaller dishes. Again, this is a really nice way to taste a variety of flavors and foods. No matter which way you enjoy these appetizers, soups and salads, I'm sure they'll be a hit.

appetizers, soups & salads

Cornmeal and Five Spice Portobella Mushrooms

This appetizer has a bit of an Asian feel to it, what with the five spice powder. It goes great with the Thai Peanut Sauce on page 84. Five spice powder can be found in any Asian market and at most grocery stores.

When you fry the mushrooms for this recipe, you only do it for a short period of time. This way you just "set" the breading, so you can finish the mushrooms in the oven later. The frying can be done several hours ahead of time.

Having your oil at the right temperature is important. If it's too cold the breading will soak up a bunch of the oil. If it's too hot the breading will burn and pull away from the mushrooms.

As far as the mushrooms go, do not rinse them in water. The texture will completely change if they are damp. You can just lightly brush off any dirt that might be on them. Besides, we all need a little dirt in our diet.

Breading ingredients:

2 cups cornmeal
2 teaspoons garlic powder
2 tablespoons five spice powder
1/2 teaspoon black pepper
1 tablespoon kosher salt

Other ingredients:

2 eggs
1 cup milk
6 portobella mushroom caps, stems removed
peanut oil for frying

Mix all the breading ingredients in a bowl until well combined. Using another bowl, whisk the eggs and milk together until well combined – this is called the egg wash. Make sure the bowls are a bit larger than needed to fit each mixture.

Bread the mushrooms one at a time in this fashion: Immerse each mushroom cap in the egg wash. Make sure the top and underside are well coated. Now lay one mushroom in the breading top side down. Shake the bowl so the breading will cover the mushroom. Press down on the mushroom so the breading adheres well. Repeat until all the mushrooms are breaded. Lay them in a single layer on a baking sheet.

To fry the mushrooms, use a deep fryer if you have one. Another way to fry them is to use a small sauté pan on the stove top. Heat the oil to 350 degrees. If you are using the sauté pan method make sure not to fill it too full, otherwise when you add the mushroom the oil will bubble up and spill over the edge. Fry each mushroom individually for about 10 to 15 seconds on each side. Remove them from the oil, drain on paper towels, and set aside in a single layer. You can now refrigerate them until needed – probably no longer than 3 or 4 hours, however.

When you are ready to bake them, just cut them into desired-size wedges. Place them on a baking sheet and bake in a preheated 400 degree oven for 15 to 20 minutes. You want them to become soft all the way through but still hold their shape.

Any leftover breading can be sifted and kept in the freezer until needed again.

Yield: 6 appetizer-size servings

Crawfish Cakes

These were one the very first menu items back when we first opened The Dining Room at 209 Main, and I thought it might be fun to revisit them. They were served with the Black Bean Vinaigrette on page 63.

I like working with crawfish for a couple reasons. First of all it's inexpensive compared to crab. Plus it's easy to work with and has its own unique flavor.

The best way to buy crawfish meat is to buy it frozen. It usually comes in one-pound packages, already out of the shell, cooked and ready to go. It can be found in most seafood stores and some Asian markets.

When the crawfish meat is thawed a bit of liquid will come out of it. In addition to that you will also want to squeeze out some more. This will keep your crawfish cakes from being too loose and they'll hold together better.

Ingredients:

1 pound thawed and squeezed crawfish meat
1/2 cup minced red bell pepper
1/2 cup minced red onion
3 cloves minced garlic
3 eggs
2 teaspoons chopped fresh thyme
1 teaspoon of your favorite bottled hot sauce
juice of 1 lime
about 1/2 cup of bread crumbs *
salt and pepper to taste
vegetable oil

The first step is to get the crawfish meat to the right consistency. Place the crawfish in a food processor and pulse until it's ground fairly fine, but not to a paste. Combine with remaining ingredients, except the vegetable oil. You want the mixture to hold together without getting too gummy. Form mixture into 2 1/2- to 3-inch cakes and set them aside.

Heat oil over medium heat in a large sauté pan. The amount of oil you need might vary. You don't want the oil to come up over the top of the cakes. You want it to just tickle the edges. The cakes will soak some of it up because of the bread crumbs.

Fry cakes in oil until browned on both sides and heated through, about 3 minutes per side. You'll probably need to do this in batches, to avoid crowding your pan. Add a little more oil as needed and reheat it between batches.

Yield: 10 to 12 cakes

* You might need more or less bread crumbs depending how much moisture is in the mixture.

Fresh Herb Cheesecake

Cheesecakes are one of the most versatile foods you can work with. Their basic ingredients are usually cream cheese, eggs, and sometimes sour cream or some other soft cheese. From there you can add whatever flavors you want.

When they hear that they are having cheesecake, most folks think of dessert, but I hope you have figured out that this is a savory cheesecake. Meaning that this makes a great appetizer as a first course or on an appetizer buffet.

One of my cheesecake techniques is to mix the ingredients by hand, rather than using an electric mixer. This will reduce the amount of air incorporated into them, and the less air, the less chance of your cake cracking while it bakes. To make the mixing easier, be sure that your ingredients (especially the cream cheese) are at room temperature and very soft.

Crust ingredients:

3/4 cup finely ground walnuts
1 cup bread crumbs
1/4 cup finely grated Parmesan
1/4 cup melted butter

Filling ingredients:

1 1/2 pounds cream cheese
6 eggs
1 cup finely grated Parmesan
juice of 1 lemon
3 tablespoons chopped fresh basil
3 tablespoons chopped fresh chives
3 tablespoons chopped fresh parsley
2 tablespoons chopped fresh thyme
salt and pepper to taste

To make crust: Combine all ingredients and press into the sides and bottom of a 10-inch spring form pan. The easiest way to do this is to start with the sides of the pan, pressing the mixture all the way to the top of the pan. If it seems like you don't have enough crust for the bottom of the pan, never fear. Take a butter knife and gently scrape some of the crust from the side. When you have enough just press it gently to the bottom.

To make the filling and bake the cheesecake: Heat oven to 300 degrees. Using a fine whisk, mix cream cheese and sour cream together until smooth. Next, whisk in the eggs, one at a time, until mixture is smooth. Use a rubber spatula to fold in the remaining ingredients until everything is well incorporated. Pour filling into crust. The filling most likely won't come to the top of the pan. Take a fork and gently knock down any crust that rises above the top of the filling. This will give you a nice decorative border around the top of the cake. Bake the cheesecake for about 1 1/2 to 2 hours. You can tell if the cake is done by gently wiggling the pan. If the center of the cake seems firm it should be done. If the cake is starting to rise in the center then it is probably past done but will still be delicious. Cool the cheesecake to room temperature then chill it thoroughly before serving.

Yield: 12 to 16 servings

Shrimp Cakes

These make a great shrimp appetizer that can be relatively inexpensive, because you can use small or broken shrimp pieces. I don't like to use the tiny "salad shrimp" as they can retain too much moisture. You most likely will be able to find some frozen broken shrimp pieces; those will work better. Of course, whole shrimp would be more than acceptable, too.

If you're cooking the shrimp yourself (as opposed to buying it already cooked), simply poach them in water over low heat. Make sure not to boil them hard or they can get rubbery. Also, they should be very well drained and completely chilled before you chop them.

Shrimp cakes taste grand with the Ginger Chimichurri on page 114. They also go well with sweet soy sauce, which is an Indonesian-style soy sauce that can be found in most Asian markets.

Ingredients:

1 pound shrimp, peeled, deveined, cooked and chilled
1/4 cup minced chives
1 tablespoon chopped cilantro
1/4 teaspoon five-spice powder
1 egg
1/3 cup bread crumbs
salt to taste
oil for sautéing

Place shrimp in a food processor and finely chop it… but don't chop it too fine or it will turn pasty. Transfer shrimp to a mixing bowl and add remaining ingredients (except oil). Mix well with a rubber spatula. Form the mixture into cakes that are 2 1/2 to 3 inches in diameter.

Heat oil in a sauté pan over medium flame. When oil is hot, add the cakes (don't crowd them in the pan, though) and sauté on each side until browned and cooked through, 3-4 minutes per side.

Yield: 6 to 8 cakes, depending on the size you prefer

Oil Rules:

When oil for sautéing is listed as an ingredient in recipes, there's no exact science for the amount to use. Different foods will absorb different amounts of oil. When you're sautéing, you can always start with a light coating of oil in the bottom of the pan and add more if the first amount becomes absorbed. Also, be sure to heat the pan and the oil before you add the food. If you put cold oil and cold food in a cold pan, you run the risk of food sticking and more oil than necessary being absorbed.

Tequila Lime Shrimp

Two of my favorite things are in this recipe: tequila and shrimp and lime and butter. OK, maybe that's more than two, but you get the point. The combination of these flavors will make you think you're on a beach in Mexico sipping margaritas, loving life, and oh yeah, eating shrimp.

In essence what you are making here is shrimp in a basic butter sauce. There are, however, a few things to watch with this recipe. First, when mincing the jalapeño wear latex gloves if you can. Note, too, that when you sauté hot peppers, they give off their oils and the air can get a little spicy. Another thing: when you add the tequila, make sure you pull your sauté pan away from the stove. Whether you have a gas or electric range, it can and most likely will flame up. Be careful!

The last thing is about the adding of the butter. If you cook the sauce too long after the butter is melted, you might have a problem; that is, the sauce can separate. You want a butter sauce to be smooth and creamy. One addition that will help prevent this is cream, which helps stabilize the sauce and creates a smoother texture. (Oh, one final note: Always remember, if you screw up a dish, never let your guests, husband/wife or mother-in-law know. Just pretend it was supposed to turn out that way.)

The dish makes a wonderful appetizer or also can be a main dish if you add a few sides. How about Jalapeño Rice (page 48), Cheddar Grits (page 57) or Chile Roasted Red Potatoes (page 46)?

Ingredients:

2 tablespoons vegetable oil
1 pound peeled, deveined medium shrimp
1 tablespoon minced jalapeño
1 bunch scallions, sliced
juice of 1 lime
1/4 cup tequila
2 tablespoons heavy cream
4 tablespoons cold butter
3 tablespoons chopped cilantro
salt

Heat oil in a large skillet over medium-high flame. Add shrimp, jalapeño and scallions. Sauté until shrimp are cooked halfway, about 2 or 3 minutes. Pull the pan away from the stove and add lime juice and tequila. Return to stove and reduce by half. Add cream and reduce by half again. Swirl in the butter until completely melted. Turn off heat and stir in cilantro. Salt to taste and serve immediately.

Yield: 6 appetizer servings

Rare-Seared Truffled Beef Bruschetta

This is a decadent style of bruschetta. You might not be into spending money on truffles or truffle oil. But if you are a real truffle fan (remember fan is short for fanatic), you are going to love this appetizer.

If you can get fresh truffles, that's great. If not, you will most likely find them canned. (And even if you don't use the entire can at one time the leftovers will freeze really well.) Another option is to just go with the oil. Also, you don't have to use the center cut of the tenderloin. You can buy some end smaller pieces, which will work just fine.

Ingredients:

10 pieces crusty French bread (sliced on the diagonal and 1-inch thick)
 extra-virgin olive oil
3/4 pound beef tenderloin, cut into pieces that are approximately 1" by 2"
1 tablespoon minced truffle
2 tablespoons balsamic vinegar
2 tablespoons truffle oil
2 tablespoons extra-virgin olive oil
1 cup seeded and diced tomato
salt and pepper to taste

Lightly oil the bread slices with olive oil on both sides and toast in 450-degree oven 5-7 minutes. Set aside.

For the beef: Heat a regular skillet (as in not a non-stick) over high flame 4-5 minutes. (This might seem a little long but you need a really hot pan. With the pan so hot the beef won't stick – mostly – so you won't need to add any oil. This also might seem strange, but with the addition of oil you run the risk of smoke and fire.)

Sear the beef on all sides for just a few seconds per side. You want to keep the meat nice and rare in the middle and also get some good color on the outside. Make sure not to crowd the beef in the pan; in fact, doing it in two batches might be the way to go. Once the beef is cool enough to handle, dice it the same size as the tomatoes. Mix beef with remaining ingredients. Spoon mixture onto the toasted bread and serve.

Yield: 10 pieces

Asian Tuna Ceviche

Here's an Asian twist on the classic Latin American ceviche. However, because you use tuna in this application, you won't soak it in the lime juice until it's completely opaque. This way it won't be "cooked" all the way through, and will still be somewhat rare – which is what you want with tuna.

On that note you might say, "How can something be 'cooked' by just sitting in lime juice?" Well, the acid in the lime juice firms up the flesh of the fish and turns it opaque (or in this case, partially opaque).

This is a great served with tortilla chips. Or, since it has the Asian twist to it you could serve it with sesame crackers or over greens as a salad.

Ingredients:

8 ounces ahi or yellowfin tuna, diced
juice of 2 limes
1 cup peeled, seeded and diced cucumber
1/4 cup diced red onion
1 clove garlic, minced
1 teaspoon minced ginger root
1 tablespoon soy sauce
1 tablespoon sesame oil
2 tablespoons chopped cilantro

Place tuna in a bowl and cover with lime juice. Don't worry if the tuna isn't completely covered, but do stir it once or twice as it marinates. Let it marinate for about 15 to 20 minutes in the refrigerator. (The longer you let it sit in the juice the more it will "cook." But if you let it sit too long the fish's flavor will be overtaken by the flavor of the lime juice.) Drain the lime juice really well from the tuna and discard the lime juice. Add the remaining ingredients to the tuna and mix well.

Yield: 4 salad portions or 16 appetizer (as in put-on-a-cracker) portions

Pepper Jack and Chèvre Queso Fundido with Crab and Roasted Sweet Corn

Many cultures have some sort of melted cheese appetizer, whether it's Swiss fondue, French brie wrapped in puff pastry, or the very American nacho cheese dip. Queso fundido is the Mexican version.

As long as you have some style of melty cheese you're good to go. In this version I use pepper jack and some fresh chèvre (soft fresh goat cheese). I also add some crab and top it with roasted sweet corn. (Delicious!)

This can be made in a single baking dish for a group or in individual casserole dishes for separate servings. Serve with tortilla chips or flour tortillas.

Ingredients:

1/2 cup (about 4 ounces) chèvre
2 cups (about 1/2 pound) grated pepper jack cheese
3/4 cup (4 ounces) crab meat
kernels from 2 ears of roasted sweet corn*

Heat oven to 400 degrees. Place chèvre in the middle of a 10-inch round baking pan (or you can use a square pan of approximately the same size). Sprinkle the pepper jack and crab over the top of the chèvre and the entire pan. Bake until cheese is melted and bubbly around the edges (around 15 to 18 minutes). Remove from oven, top with sweet corn and serve.

Yield: 4 to 6 servings

* The easiest way to roast corn is to leave it on the (shucked) cob and place it directly over the burner of a gas stove. You just want to get a little bit of color on the kernels. Some would say it looks like they are slightly burned. This just adds a little more flavor to the whole dish. This method will also burn off any of the silk that might be left behind.

Mothers

Shortly after Jane and I moved to Green County, Jane's mother Ruth followed us here and bought a place of her own. When the restaurant was in its infancy we asked my mother Pat if she would be able to help out and wait tables once in a while. She was a seasoned veteran and, lucky for us, she accepted.

Soon Pat was working once or twice a week while still living north of Madison. Well, that didn't last long. Pat and her husband George made the move south and all of the sudden we were living within a mile or two of both our mothers.

Some couples might cringe at the thought; however, it worked out very nicely indeed. For example, Ruth, being our landlord for the restaurant, was within earshot if the furnace broke down. And if we needed the dogs to be let out, Pat was available.

Okay, those aren't the only reasons we like having them around. They are both integral parts of the restaurant. Ruth is an avid knitter and has many connections in the textile world. She helps to coordinate the textile shows that are displayed at the restaurant, and is always happy to engage in conversation with guests and tell them about the textiles.

"Who was that sassy waiter?" guests will ask. Well, that's my mom. She tells it like she sees it, and really likes to have fun with the guests, if they'll engage. She is a great promoter of the restaurant (could be she likes the chef) and will convince you to have dessert even if you don't want one.

Beer and Cheese Soup

It seems that a good amount of Wisconsin restaurants have their version of this soup, so here is mine. You can use any cheese or cheeses you want, but good old Cheddar works just fine. Ham or sausage are also great additions.

It might seem like the recipe uses a lot of oil to sauté the vegetables, but with the addition of the flour later on you are actually making a roux to thicken the soup.

You could also call this cheese and beer soup, but I like to put my favorite ingredient first.

Ingredients:

1/2 cup vegetable oil
1 cup diced onion
2 cloves minced garlic
1 cup diced red pepper
1/2 cup flour
4 cups chicken stock
1 1/3 cups heavy cream
1 can or bottle (12 ounces) of your favorite beer (Yum!)
1 teaspoon smoked sweet paprika
1/3 pound grated cheese (about 2 1/2 cups)
salt and pepper

Heat oil in a heavy pot over medium heat. Add the onion, garlic and red pepper and sauté until veggies are almost cooked through. Be careful not to get the oil too hot and "fry" the veggies.

Whisk in the flour until smooth. Slowly add the stock while whisking the veggie mixture. (The whisking action is very important – it helps prevent the formation of little, not-so-tasty roux dumplings.) Bring to a boil so the roux will thicken the soup to its fullest potential. Add the cream, beer and paprika. Bring to a boil again, add the cheese and whisk until melted. Remove from heat and salt and pepper to taste.

Yield: 8 cups

BLACK BEAN AND CHORIZO SOUP

Soup is one of the types of food that's easy to put your signature on. This one, for instance, has a Southwestern/Mexican feel to it; for my own personal touch I would add either some chipotle peppers or some roasted poblanos. If you don't care for too much heat yourself, some red bell pepper could be added for extra flavor. The chorizo could be substituted by chicken or pork. And the fun part is what you garnish your soup with: roasted sweet corn, sour cream, Smoked Tomato Remoulade (see recipe on page 86), crispy tortilla strips – the possibilities are endless.

Now let's talk about the chorizo. If you have worked with chorizo before you know it has lots of fat and that it is very crumbly when cooked. (Mexican-style chorizo, that is; Spanish chorizo is a firm-textured cured sausage.) There is a way around those. When you buy chorizo it usually comes in plastic casing. From here I like to leave the chorizo in its casing and slowly poach it in water until cooked through. Next, completely cool it. From there just remove it from the casing, get rid of the solidified fat, and slice the sausage into disks.

If you like to leave the fat in and are fine with chorizo crumbles, simply forget the few seconds of your life you just wasted reading the previous sentences.

INGREDIENTS:

2 tablespoons vegetable oil
1 1/2 cups diced onion
6 cloves minced garlic
1 1/2 tablespoons ground cumin
1 teaspoon ground coriander
2 cups chopped tomatoes (fresh or canned)
2 cups cooked black beans
4 cups stock (homemade or canned)
1 pound raw chorizo (or the cooked product from 1 pound)
salt and pepper

Heat oil in a heavy pot over medium heat. Add the onion and garlic and sauté the mixture for several minutes. This is the point you would add your raw chorizo if you're using that, and sauté it until cooked through. Add the cumin and coriander and sauté for 20 to 30 seconds longer. Now add tomatoes, beans and stock, and simmer for about 20 to 30 minutes. If you cooked the chorizo ahead of time add it now and simmer for just a few more minutes. Add salt and pepper to taste, and garnish to your heart's content.

Yield: 8 to 10 cups

Three Mushroom Sherry Soup

Any of your favorite mushrooms will work for this unless your favorite mushroom is a truffle. Then it could get a little expensive.

You can either leave this as a brothy soup or thicken it slightly with a little cornstarch or arrowroot mixed with water or broth.

Ingredients:

3 tablespoons vegetable oil
1 cup minced onion
4 cloves garlic, minced
2 cups sliced shiitake mushrooms
2 cups sliced portobella mushrooms
2 cups sliced button mushrooms
1 cup dry sherry
2 tablespoons fresh chopped thyme
4 cups chicken or vegetable broth
salt and pepper

Heat oil in a heavy pot over medium heat, add onions and garlic, and sauté for several minutes. Add the mushrooms and sauté until they start to cook down and release some liquid. Add the sherry and thyme, bring to a simmer, and cook until the liquid reduces by half. Add the stock and simmer 20 to 25 minutes. Add salt and pepper to taste. This is the point that you could thicken the soup if you choose.

Yield: 7 to 8 cups

Thai Curry Coconut Soup

This is a Thai-style curry soup made with store-bought curry paste, an ingredient that is usually found in small tin cans or plastic containers. It comes in red or green, and I think the red is a little spicier.

A few other ingredients might be hard to find, unless you have access to a really nice Asian market. The galanga root looks similar to ginger, but has a spicy and fruitier flavor. The inside tender layers of the lemongrass are the ones you want in this preparation because they aren't as fibrous as the outer layers.

Using regular coconut milk as opposed to light is pretty crucial to this soup. The regular style really helps with the texture and thickness.

The turmeric is for aesthetic purposes only. It will give the soup a lovely yellow color. As we all know, even great-tasting food has to look good, too.

Ingredients:

- 2 tablespoons vegetable oil
- 1 1/2 cups diced onion
- 1 1/2 cups diced red bell pepper
- 6 cloves garlic, minced
- 2 tablespoons minced ginger root
- 2 tablespoons minced galanga root
- 2 tablespoons minced lemongrass
- 1 1/2 teaspoons red curry paste
- 1/4 cup fresh lime juice
- 1 teaspoon turmeric
- 4 cans (each 13 ounces) coconut milk
- 1/3 cup chopped cilantro
- salt

Heat oil in a heavy pot over medium flame. Add onion, pepper, garlic, galanga, ginger root and lemongrass. Sauté for several minutes, making sure not to get any color on the veggies. Add curry paste, lime juice, turmeric and coconut milk. Bring to a boil and reduce to a simmer for 20-30 minutes. Add salt to taste. Divide soup into serving bowls and garnish with fresh cilantro. Enjoy.

Yield: 8 servings

Tomato and Red Pepper Bisque

I developed this soup for one of my cooking classes several years ago. One of the great things to come out of teaching classes is recipe development. Another is that I get to meet many new people and make some new friends.

This is a pretty straightforward purée-type soup that's ideal for a brunch item or for lunch or a work break on a cold winter afternoon. I like to strain it after it's puréed – to get it extra-smooth – although that's up to you. You might want to dice all of the vegetables and leave it chunky. Another addition to this, beyond tomatoes and red peppers, could be some cooked shrimp or crab.

Ingredients:

2 tablespoons olive oil
1 sliced onion, sliced
4 cloves garlic, chopped
2 cups red bell peppers, sliced
2 cups chopped canned or very ripe fresh tomatoes
2 cups water
1 cup heavy cream
1/4 cup packed fresh basil leaves
salt and pepper

Heat oil in a soup pot over low flame. Add onions, garlic and peppers and sauté until vegetables are cooked through. Make sure not to get any color or browning on the veggies. Add tomatoes, cream and water and simmer 15-20 minutes. Add basil and purée until smooth. Strain through a fine sieve until all the moisture is pushed through the sieve. Add salt and pepper to taste.

Yield: About 6 cups

Cooking Classes

Because we are located in the middle of a pretty rural area in Wisconsin, life can get a little lonely during winter in the restaurant business. I think it was the second winter we were open when we didn't know if we should clean the ceiling again or count the snowflakes on the front sidewalk. We needed to do something.

I had a chef friend in Madison who was teaching cooking classes at the time and he suggested we try them. I'd never taught a class before, but we gave it a whirl to keep us busy through the winter months.

The first year was a small success, and the next was even better. We just finished our eleventh year of classes and the response to them has been amazing to me. Not that people are standing in line to get into a class, but pretty darn close.

A few nice perks resulted from the classes. First, teaching has helped me expand my knowledge of food, and some of what I learned – and then taught to others – ended up on the menu (and in this book). Even better has been the people. We have met so many interesting folks through the classes and a good number of them have become friends. And a good number of them also have memberships at private golf courses that they have taken us to. Now that's what I call a perk.

CHIPOTLE CAESAR DRESSING

One of my favorite salads is the classic Caesar. I love the saltiness of the anchovies – there can never be too many extra on top of my Caesar. I remember as a child my mother would bring out a teak salad bowl set and make the real deal. She would rub the bowl with garlic cloves and mash the anchovies and make the salad right in the bowl.

Well, times have changed and I don't have a teak salad bowl set, so here is my version with a twist. As you might have noticed I really like to use chipotle peppers. The canned ones are the easiest to use and add some nice spice and smoke to the dressing.*

Instead of making it by hand in a salad bowl, I use a blender. This is basically a vinaigrette; the blending holds the oil and other liquids together.

INGREDIENTS:

juice of 2 lemons
1 egg
6 anchovy fillets
1 tablespoon Worcestershire sauce
2 cloves garlic
1 teaspoon canned chipotle peppers
1 cup pure olive oil
salt

Place lemon juice, egg, anchovies, Worcestershire, garlic and chipotle in a blender. Blend on high until well puréed. Keep the machine going as you slowly drizzle in the olive oil until completely incorporated. Add salt to taste. Because anchovies are already salty you might not need to add any salt at all.

Refrigerate dressing until ready to use.

Yield: 3/4 cups

*To store extra chipotles left in the can, lay them in a single layer on waxed paper. Make sure they aren't touching. Place the paper in the freezer on a level surface. When the peppers are frozen, just put them in a zipper bag or plastic container and then you can use one at a time when needed.

Ginger Miso Peanut Dressing

Miso is an aged soy bean paste that is used in traditional Japanese cooking. It is made from barley and rice and comes in light and dark – the light type is sweeter in flavor while the dark is saltier and more intensely flavored.

This dressing can be made like a vinaigrette by adding the oil last to help keep the dressing from separating… although the peanut butter and the miso give it enough body to prevent that from happening. I really like this dressing on heartier type greens like cabbage or bok choy. It can also be a great dipping sauce for raw veggies.

Ingredients:

2 tablespoons minced ginger root
2 tablespoons light miso
1/4 cup creamy peanut butter
1 tablespoon soy sauce
1/2 cup rice vinegar
3/4 cup pure olive oil

Place first five ingredients in a blender and purée well. With the machine running, slowly add the olive oil until it's fully incorporated. This will keep in the refrigerator for several weeks.

Yield: 1 3/4 cups

Chilled Salmon Salad with Indian Curry Vinaigrette

Any cooked and chilled seafood will be good in this vibrant salad. At the restaurant we use salmon because its flavor and texture seem to work particularly well with the other ingredients. This makes a great starter salad, or double it up for a nice lunch entrée.

There are a couple different ways to cook the salmon before chilling it. One way is to bake the salmon in the oven until is just cooked through, and then chill it in the refrigerator. Once it's cooled you can either flake it or cut it up into desired sized pieces.

The second way is to dice the salmon when it's raw and poach it lightly in water until just cooked. The pieces will take about 7 to 9 minutes to poach. Then you can strain them and rinse under cold water. The rinsing is important because a lot of the fat will come out in the poaching process, so you want to get that off the cooked fish.

Ingredients:

1/2 pound (about 2 cups) diced, cooked salmon
2 cups peeled, seeded and diced cucumber
1 tablespoon chopped fresh mint
3/4 cup Indian Curry Vinaigrette (see page 87)
salt and pepper
5 cups baby spinach (about 5 ounces)

Mix salmon, cucumber, mint and vinaigrette until well coated. Add salt and pepper to taste. Divide spinach among four plates and top with salmon salad. If this is for a summer meal, don't forget the Champagne.

Yield: 4 servings

Our House Salad Dressing

This is the house dressing recipe we have used since day one. It's a straightforward vinaigrette with some fresh basil and lemon balm added. The balsamic vinegar also gives it unique flavor.

The use of the blender will help to emulsify all the ingredients. What this means is it will help to keep the oil and vinegar combined. The egg will also help with this process, although that's optional.

If you don't have lemon balm available you can use the juice of 1/2 of a lemon.

Because of the high acidity from the vinegar this dressing will keep for quite a while in the refrigerator.

Note that I list pure olive oil – the reason being that when refrigerated it won't solidify like extra virgin can. We all know about those extra virgins.

Ingredients:

1/3 cup packed fresh basil leaves
1/4 cup packed fresh lemon balm leaves
2 cloves garlic
1/2 cup balsamic vinegar
1 raw egg
1 cup pure olive oil (or your favorite light oil)

Purée basil, lemon balm, garlic, vinegar, and egg in a blender. Keep blender running on high speed while you slowly add the oil until fully incorporated.

Yield: 1 1/4 cups

Italian Bread Salad

Not only does this taste good, but its colors are wonderful too. This is a salad you can play with as far as the ingredients go. Throw some roasted red peppers or artichoke hearts in if you want to.

The texture of the bread is key for this recipe. I like a pretty heavy, crusty-style bread, something along the lines of a sourdough. If you mix the salad together too far in advance the bread can start to get soggy; that's why I like the hearty bread, because it holds up longer. You'll also want to toast it, and the easiest way to do several slices at once is in a 400-degree oven for about 5 to 7 minutes.

DRESSING INGREDIENTS:

1 clove garlic
1/4 cup grated Parmesan
1/4 cup chopped fresh parsley
1/2 cup chopped fresh basil
2 tablespoons lemon juice
3 tablespoons rice vinegar
1/4 cup virgin olive oil
salt and pepper to taste

SALAD INGREDIENTS:

1 can (14 ounces) cannellini beans, drained
8 cherry tomatoes, quartered
1 cup peeled, seeded and sliced cucumber
1/2 cup whole pitted Kalamata olives
1/4 cup toasted pine nuts
3 cups cubed and lightly toasted crusty bread
1/2 cup grated Parmesan cheese

To make the dressing: Purée all the ingredients in a blender until smooth. (Even though this is a vinaigrette style dressing you don't have to add the oil last, as is typical. The large amount of herbs and the cheese help to hold it together.)

To make the salad: Combine beans, tomatoes, cucumber, olives, pine nuts and bread with the dressing. Stir until well coated and top with Parmesan.

Yield: 4 to 6 servings

Poppy Seed Fennel Slaw

I love slaw, and I think cabbage is to a slaw dressing just what French fries are to ketchup. They both taste good by themselves, but are a great vehicle for some wonderful sauce.

This slaw recipe features some fresh fennel and poppy seeds, for a little different flavor. And note: Even though it might look like quite a bit of cabbage and fennel to start, once all the ingredients are combined they will all settle in together and nestle down into a delicious flavor combination.

Ingredients:

1 clove garlic, minced and mashed
1/3 cup rice vinegar
1/3 cup extra virgin olive oil
2 teaspoons celery salt
1 tablespoon poppy seeds
1/2 teaspoon black pepper
3 cups thinly sliced fennel bulb
3 cups thinly sliced purple cabbage
3 cups thinly sliced green cabbage

Combine all ingredients in a large bowl. Let stand in refrigerator for at least 30 minutes for flavors to come together. However, note that the longer it sits, the more tender the cabbage and fennel will get. So if you desire a crispier style slaw, serve it soon after the ingredients are combined.

Yield: 6 to 8 servings

Side Dishes

The right sides with a meal are just as important as the other components of a meal, especially here in Wisconsin, we really enjoy our mashed potatoes.

Well, these recipes aren't just mashed potatoes, except for the mashed potatoes. Seriously though I like to have a variety of side dishes in my arsenal to keep things interesting.

These are mostly starch type dishes, but they can still be really versatile with different styles of food. The Cheddar grits or sweet corn bread pudding are great additions to a Southwestern style cuisine while the Parmesan risotto goes really well with seafood.

However you mash it, bake it or roast it make sure you enjoy the experience and the leftovers.

side dishes

Butternut Squash Risotto

This isn't your traditional-style risotto, mostly because the star here is the squash and not necessarily the rice. With that in mind we need to talk about the squash.

There are a two ways to cook the squash. The first, and the way I like to do it, is to cut the squash in half lengthwise and scoop out the seeds and guts. From here lay it flat side down on a baking sheet and bake in 350-degree oven for about 1 1/4 to 1 3/4 hours, depending on the size of the squash. It is done when the squash is soft and the skin is kind of wrinkled.

The second way is to peel the squash when it's raw, scoop out the seeds and guts and cut it into chunks. Now you just simmer it in some water until the squash is soft. I don't like this method as much because the flavor of the squash can get diluted from the water.

The Gruyère cheese at the end will give it just a little bit of a distinctive flavor (but Parmesan would also work). This is a great side dish, and it could also work as a main course, along with some sautéed spinach and toasted pumpkin seeds.

Ingredients:

2 tablespoons vegetable oil
1/2 cup minced onion
1 cup Arborio rice
2 cups vegetable broth
1/2 cup dry white wine
2 cups cooked and puréed butternut squash*
1 cup grated Gruyère cheese
salt and pepper

Heat oil in a heavy pot over medium heat. Add onions and sauté for about a minute. Add the rice and sauté for another minute or two, stirring occasionally. Turn the heat down to low and add the broth and wine in several batches. You want to make sure that almost all of the moisture is absorbed between each batch and that you are stirring it pretty frequently. Once most of the moisture is absorbed you can add the squash. Turn the heat up to about medium and stir it really well until the squash is hot. Add the cheese and stir until melted. Remove from heat and add salt and pepper to taste.

Yield: about 6 cups

*If you have any squash leftover it will freeze really well.

Roasted Vegetable Caponata

Although this isn't a traditional caponata, it's a version that has several applications. (That's one of the nice things about food and recipes, you can put your own twist, variation, or interpretation on a dish and call it whatever you want to.) This can be served hot or cold, as a side dish, or with some crackers or pita bread as an appetizer.

The length of the roasting time is the key to the flavor and texture of this dish. You'll want to make sure you get some good "color" on the vegetables, which can be mistaken as burned. Some of the veggies around the edge of the pan may get a little crispy and might need to be tossed. Letting everything sit together for a day after the roasting really helps the flavors come together.

To roast the garlic, place the peeled cloves in a small, heavy-bottomed sauce pan and barely cover them with olive oil. Roast over low heat until cloves are soft. This should take about 20 to 30 minutes. Make sure not to cook at too high of a temperature or the garlic will get sticky and be too firm. You can then use the oil that's left for future batches of caponata or other sautéing applications.

Ingredients:

4 cups diced eggplant
3 cups diced zucchini
2 cups diced red bell pepper
1 cup diced red onion
1/4 cup olive oil
1/3 cup balsamic vinegar
1/2 cup roasted garlic cloves
1/4 cup pitted and chopped Kalamata olives
2 tablespoons capers
1/4 cup chopped fresh basil
salt and pepper to taste

Mix first six ingredients together in a bowl and spread in an even layer on an oiled 12 by 18-inch sheet pan. Roast in a preheated 400-degree oven for about 1 1/4 to 1 1/2 hours, stirring halfway through. The roasting time may vary depending on what size you cut your vegetables, so always check them early.

When veggies get some of that good color on them, remove from oven and let cool to room temperature. Once cooled, mix them with the remaining ingredients. For best flavor, store in the refrigerator in a covered container overnight.

If you are going to serve this as a hot dish just reheat in the microwave or on the stove top over low heat.

Yield: Six 1/2-cup servings

CHILE-ROASTED RED POTATOES

It's always fun to mess around with different ingredients. And when I'm doing that, my love for Southwestern flavors seems to show up more often than not. This is a simple Southwestern-style side dish that goes great with grilled foods or anything kind of summery.

I really like using red potatoes for roasting. They hold their shape really well and can even get a nice kind of crust on the outside. Make sure not to crowd the potatoes too much on the baking pan. This can make them retain moisture and they'll end up soggy.

INGREDIENTS:

2 pounds small red potatoes
1 tablespoon smoked sweet paprika*
1 tablespoon chile powder
1 1/2 tablespoons olive oil
salt to taste

Heat oven to 400 degrees. Cut potatoes in quarters and mix with remaining ingredients. Place in a single layer on an oiled baking sheet and bake until cooked through and tender, stirring once half way through the cooking time. It will take a total of about 50 minutes, but cooking times are not always exact and it depends on the oven you have and the doneness you prefer. Some people like their potatoes a little on the firm side while others may want them cooked through completely.

*This paprika is pretty mainstream and can be found in the spice section of your local store.

Yield: 6 to 8 servings

SWEET CORN BREAD PUDDING

No summertime cookout would be complete without this wonderful savory cornbread pudding. With jack cheese and cumin, it's got a bit of a Southwestern feel to it.

It doesn't matter if you make your own cornbread or use a store-bought mix – you will still come out with a great side dish. You can also use frozen or canned corn if fresh isn't available. Just make sure it's drained really well.

INGREDIENTS:

4 cups cubed cornbread
2 cups sweet corn kernels
1 1/2 cups diced red bell pepper
1 bunch sliced green onions
2 cups grated jack cheese
6 eggs
2 1/2 cups buttermilk
1 tablespoon cumin
2 teaspoons salt

Combine first five ingredients in a large bowl. Make sure not to mix too vigorously or the cornbread might crumble. Using a separate bowl, whisk together the eggs, buttermilk, cumin, and salt. Pour egg mixture over cornbread mixture and stir gently. Pour into a greased 9 by 13-inch baking dish. Let mixture stand for 1/2 hour so the cornbread can soak up some of the moisture. Meanwhile, heat oven to 350 degrees. Bake cornbread 1 hour. Serve warm or at room temperature.

Yield: 10 to 12 servings

JALAPENO RICE

Here is a simple yet flavorful rice dish that goes well with many meats and seafood. If you are serving it with seafood, you can substitute Shrimp Stock (see page 103) or bottled clam juice for the chicken stock.

I really like to use basmati rice instead of "regular" long-grain rice – it's more fragrant and delicate. It does have a little different liquid-to-rice ratio than regular rice. Note that rinsing basmati in a sieve under cold water will remove a good amount of the starch. This will keep the rice from sticking together.

INGREDIENTS:

2 tablespoons vegetable oil
2 cloves garlic, minced
1/2 teaspoon ground cumin
1 tablespoon minced canned jalapeño pepper
1 cup basmati rice, rinsed
1 1/4 cups chicken stock (homemade or canned)
1/3 cup tomato juice

Heat oil in a heavy saucepan over low flame. Add garlic and sauté it for just a minute, making sure it doesn't start to brown. Add remaining ingredients, stir well and bring to a boil over high heat. Turn heat down to low and cover the pan. Cook the rice until almost all of the liquid is absorbed, about 8 to 10 minutes. Remove from heat and let stand for several minutes until all of the liquid is absorbed.

Yield: 2 1/2 cups

Creamy Parmesan Risotto

The classic way to get a nice creamy risotto is to take your time adding the liquid to the rice. That way the starch from the rice is slowly released and gives it that creamy texture. But here we're also going to going to cheat a little, by adding cream and some Parmesan.

This is a great side dish with chicken, or as an appetizer. If you substituted shellfish stock for the chicken stock, this would also work with seafood.

Ingredients:

2 tablespoons vegetable oil
3/4 cup diced red bell pepper
1 cup Arborio rice
2 cups chicken stock
1/2 cup heavy cream
3/4 cup grated Parmesan
salt and pepper

Heat oil in a heavy sauce pan over medium flame. Add the diced red pepper and rice and sauté the mixture for 1 to 2 minutes. Turn heat down to low and begin to add stock and cream about 1/2 cup at a time. After each addition of liquid, stir the rice until almost all of the liquid is absorbed. Once all of the liquid is absorbed, the rice is barely tender and the risotto has a creamy texture, add the cheese, salt and pepper to taste. Stir until cheese is melted. Serve it right away. Or, if you're not serving it right away, it can be reheated gently over low heat. You might need to add a little water to get it back to its creamy consistency.

Yield: 6 to 8 side dish servings

Mashed Potatoes

When I was deciding what recipes to put in this book, mashed potatoes never crossed my mind. Everyone knows how to make mashed potatoes, don't they? Then I realized that just because something seems basic and easy to prepare doesn't mean that everyone knows how to do it. So here is my version of one of the world's most delicious foods.

Since the main ingredient in mashed potatoes is potatoes, that ingredient should be the most important. Even though I'm a Wisconsin boy, Idaho's Burbank russet potatoes are the best for this application. On the other hand some good old fashioned Wisconsin cream is a key ingredient, also. Not milk: cream.

For the mashing part of the recipe, I like to just use a heavy whisk. Some people use an electric mixer, or you could be really crazy and use an old-fashioned potato masher. It's up to you.

Ingredients:

5 medium Idaho potatoes, about 3 pounds total
1/4 pound (1 stick) unsalted butter, cubed and brought to room temperature
2/3 cup warmed heavy cream
salt and pepper

Peel potatoes and cut them into about 2-inch chunks. Place them in a heavy pot and cover with water. Bring to a boil and then turn them down to a simmer. If you boil the potatoes the whole time they will disintegrate. Cook until tender – this means you can easily cut one with a fork. Drain potatoes in a sieve. Let them sit in the sieve for about 30 or 40 seconds. This will assure that all the water is drained. Place them back in the pot and add the butter. Commence with the mashing, using your favorite mashing implement, until the butter is melted. Add the cream and mix until incorporated. Add salt and pepper to taste.

Yield: 6 to 8 servings, unless your diners are mashed potato fiends; then this might be only 3 or 4 servings.

Herb-Mashed Red Potatoes

This is a simple twist on good ol' mashed potatoes. I like to use red potatoes here so I can leave the skin on them when they get mashed. As you can see, I am not a mashed potato purist. Even with potato mashing equipment, in fact. Some folks like to use a potato ricer, some a good old-fashioned potato masher, and some an electric mixer. For this preparation I prefer a sturdy slotted spoon so as to mash them well but also leave them chunky.

Ingredients:

1 1/2 pounds red potatoes
4 tablespoons unsalted butter
1/2 cup heavy cream
2 tablespoons chopped fresh parsley
2 tablespoons chopped fresh basil
2 tablespoons chopped fresh chives
2 tablespoons chopped fresh thyme
salt and pepper

Place potatoes in a heavy pot and cover with water. Make sure the pot is deep enough so the water will cover the potatoes and then some. Bring to a boil over high heat and then turn down to a simmer. You want to make sure the potatoes cook all the way through but don't disintegrate from vigorous boiling. This will take about 20 to 30 minutes, depending on the size of the potatoes. To check if they are done, place a potato on a counter top or cutting board and gently press it with the back of a spoon. If it smashes easily, then you're in business.

Drain the potatoes well and return them to the pot they were cooked in. Add the butter, cream and herbs and mix/smash them with a sturdy slotted spoon until the butter is melted. Add the salt and pepper to taste and enjoy.

Yield: 4 to 6 servings

Parmesan Polenta

There are several schools of thought when it comes to polenta. I've seen many recipes that call for constant and continuous stirring for quite a while. My thought is a little different. I prepare polenta similar to the way you make grits: when the liquid is absorbed it's ready to go.

I like to use milk in polenta, because milk makes it nice and creamy, but chicken or vegetable broth also work well. In this recipe you'll be using some Parmesan cheese to boost the flavor a bit. Other cheeses could also be used, such as Cheddar, smoked cheeses or chèvre.

Although regular fine ground cornmeal works for this recipe, the coarse ground really gives it a whole different texture: gutsier, more interesting… makes your mouth stand up and take notice.

This polenta makes a great vegetarian entrée or appetizer when topped with the Roasted Vegetable Caponata on page 44. It's also nice with the Roasted Garlic Cream Sauce on page 72.

Ingredients:

3 cups milk
1 teaspoon garlic powder
salt
1 1/2 cups coarse ground polenta cornmeal
1 1/2 cups grated Parmesan cheese

Lightly oil a sheet pan with 1-inch sides and set it aside. Place milk, garlic powder and salt in a heavy sauce pan and bring to a boil over high heat. (The amount of salt you add is up to your own personal taste. Remember that the cheese most likely has some salt in it.)

Once the milk boils, turn it down to low heat and whisk in the polenta. Make sure that there aren't any lumps. Once the mixture starts to thicken you want to change from a whisk to a spoon. Otherwise you might get a big glob of polenta stuck in the middle of your whisk.

Now stir in the cheese until it's completely melted. While the mixture is still warm, spread it out onto the prepared pan into an even layer that's about 1 inch thick – if the pan is large the mixture might cover the entire surface. Refrigerate until polenta is cool and firm.

Now comes the fun part. Heat oven to 425 degrees. Unmold the polenta from the pan and cut into squares or triangles or circles or bunnies… or whatever shape you want. Place the polenta pieces back onto the same oiled pan, evenly spaced apart. Bake until the pieces are heated through and their undersides are golden, about 15 minutes.

Yield: 8 servings

Zucchini Potato Pancakes

This is a little twist on your everyday potato pancake recipe. Most everyone has their own recipe that they got from their grandmother or mom. If you use my recipe hopefully I'll rank right up there with Grandma.

Getting rid of most of the moisture in the potatoes and zucchini is key to this recipe. If you don't get rid of the moisture it will come out in the pancake mixture (read: soupy pancake mixture). And time is critical. Don't let the grated veggies sit around; you need to get to them quickly or they will turn gray in color and won't look very appetizing.

The easiest way to get rid of the moisture involves a kitchen towel or large cloth napkin. Make sure you don't use the good holiday snowman hand towel or there may be a price to pay. Grate the potatoes and zucchini and place them in a bowl. You will start to see quite a bit of liquid coming out of them right away. Lay the towel flat on the counter and place a baseball sized handful in the middle of the towel. Now gather up the corners together and twist the towel. The pressure from the twisting will force the liquid out. You might be able to use the liquid for another purpose, but I usually just toss it.

These can make a great appetizer or entrée. Just top with some sour cream and crumbled aged Cheddar and you might forget your grandmother could ever cook.

Ingredients:

1 pound Yukon Gold potatoes (or your favorite type of potatoes)
1 pound zucchini
1/2 cup minced red onion
3 tablespoons chopped fresh basil
2 eggs
1/4 cup flour
salt and pepper
vegetable oil for sautéing

Grate the potatoes and zucchini with a coarse cheese grater. Squeeze out the liquid as explained above. Now mix them together with the onion, basil, egg and flour. Add salt and pepper to taste. Form the mixture into the size of cakes that you want. Heat the oil in a non-stick sauté pan over medium heat. Place your cakes in the pan and cook on each side until browned and cooked through.

The raw mixture can't really sit around for too long or it will start to gray. The cooked pancakes, however, can be cooked ahead of time and reheated in the oven.

Yield: 4 entrée portions or 8 appetizer portions

Cheddar Grits

Grits are something that some folks associate with the mushy, flavorless breakfast food that Mom used to serve when they were young. (Mom, I forgive you.) This version is a great side dish that is nice and creamy and cheesy. You can also add a little cumin and jalapeño to give it a Southwestern feel and flavor. We even have some guests at the restaurant who order them to go so they can fry them up for breakfast the next morning with a couple of poached eggs.

For a creamy texture, serve these grits right after cooking them. Or they can be made the day ahead and reheated for something a little firmer, with more of a polenta texture. For the cheese, I use regular medium Cheddar; however, feel free to use a sharp Cheddar – or even a smoked Cheddar works nicely.

Ingredients:

2 1/2 cups milk
1 teaspoon garlic powder
just shy of 2/3 cup quick-cooking grits
4 ounces (about 1 cup) grated Cheddar cheese
salt

In a heavy bottom sauce pan bring the milk and garlic powder to a boil. Turn down to a simmer and slowly whisk in the grits. Make sure to use a whisk or you could get lumpy grits. Stir occasionally until they start to thicken. Add the cheese and stir until melted. Stir in salt to taste. Once the milk boils it should take about 5 to 8 minutes to cook the grits. They will also thicken upon standing if you make them ahead and hold them warm.

Yield: 5 to 6 servings

Our Staff

We are the luckiest restaurant owners in the world. (Well, at least in Monticello, Wisconsin.) Our staff rarely turns over. Our waiter Lori has been with us since day one. Our newest waiter was hired ten years ago.

What keeps them with us? I like to think that they just like us, which could be part of it. The real reasons I believe are pretty down-to-earth. We have created a really nice work environment where we treat the teenagers like adults, so hopefully they will treat us the same. And the adults get free Schlitz at the end of their shift if they want. There are no kitchen-versus-wait staff feuds. Jane and I own the place, but we also work alongside our staff.

There is quite an age difference among the staff, for it is made up of mostly teenagers and grandmothers. There are a few exceptions, those being the middle-agers. With that said, even though there is a generation gap or two, everyone gets along. Some of the kids will come over to our house to watch a football game and hang out with us like we are normal people, not weird adults.

For instance, my sous chef Jimmy and I go to Las Vegas every year, even though he's young enough to be my son. Also when we have our employee holiday party we all interact together even though there is that age difference thing. We are like a family – we like to be around each other, just maybe not for prolonged periods of time.

Sauces

Hurray, sauces! I love love love sauces, mostly because I think this is my strong point in cooking. Sauces to me are one of the most wonderful and interesting aspects of the culinary world.

I will use the word "sauce" in several different contexts throughout these recipes. A sauce can be a thin broth, or it can be thickened with a roux, or thickened with a purée of its own ingredients. Or, a sauce can be reduced to produce a rich delicious complement that will really set a dish apart from others. I've included a special section devoted just to the reduction sauces.

sauces

CREAMY AVOCADO SAUCE

This is a sauce that can be used on tacos or as a dip for vegetables. And it's really wonderful on the roasted Roasted Vegetable Taco Filling on page 148.

It's best to make this in a small food processor or blender so everything gets puréed really well.

INGREDIENTS:

1 avocado
juice of 1/2 lime
1 clove garlic, minced
1 heaping tablespoon cilantro leaves
1/2 teaspoon ground cumin
1/2 cup sour cream
1/4 cup water
salt to taste

Peel avocado and remove pit. Place avocado flesh and lime juice in a food processor and purée well. (This helps the sauce keep its nice green color longer.) Add remaining ingredients and purée until smooth.

Yield: 1 1/2 cups

BLACK BEAN VINAIGRETTE

Even though I really love reduction sauces, there is something about really simple cold sauces that also does it for me.

This is not really a traditional vinaigrette, but it has vinegar in it, so there you go. The sauce works well with the Crawfish Cakes on page 8, the Shrimp Cakes on page 12, or any type of seafood that needs a dipping sauce.

Feel free to use canned black beans as long they're drained really well. You can also cook dried ones if you want.

INGREDIENTS:

1/2 cup cooked black beans
2 tablespoons cider vinegar
1 teaspoon ground cumin
about 1/2 cup water
salt

Purée all ingredients in a blender adding salt to taste at the end. You might need to add more or less water depending on what consistency you desire.

Yield: 1 1/4 cups

Blue Cheese Cream Sauce

I really like to make simple cold sauces as accompaniments to various dishes. A lot of the time they're dairy-based, as in milk, heavy cream or sour cream. I think these types of sauces can really elevate certain dishes to another level of not only flavor and texture, but also appearance.

Although I call this a "cream" sauce, no cream was harmed in the making of this sauce. (I used milk instead of cream because the cream would whip before the cheese purées.) It's delicious with steaks, or could be used as a vegetable dip, or even thinned out and used as a dressing for salads.

Note that some blue cheeses will be firmer than others so you might need to adjust the thickness of your sauce depending on the brand of cheese you use. Also, I've listed the cheese in weight instead of volume because I think it's a little tough to measure crumbled cheese that way. If you don't have a scale, just look at the weight on the package and use what you need.

Ingredients:

1/2 cup milk
6 ounces crumbled blue cheese

Place milk and cheese in a blender and purée until smooth. Small batches of liquids are hard to purée in some blenders because their design allows too much air in the bottom of the pitcher, which keeps you from getting that nice vortex in the blender. One way to prevent this is to make a larger batch or you could use an emersion blender.

Yield: 1 cup

ROASTED TOMATO CHIPOTLE KETCHUP

Okay, this really isn't the ketchup you would find in the store, but it's really tasty and gives you an excuse to eat more French fries.

I like to use rice vinegar in this because it's not as acidic as some vinegars. Plus there is already some acidity from the roasted tomatoes.

INGREDIENTS:

1 cup Oven Roasted Tomatoes (recipe on page 116)
1/4 cup rice vinegar
1 1/2 teaspoons canned chipotle peppers
1/4 cup water
salt

Purée first four ingredients in a food processor or blender. You might need to add a little more water if you want it thinner. Strain through a sieve, making sure to push all the liquid that you can through. Discard the skin and seeds from the sieve. Add salt to taste… and fire up the deep fryer for those French fries!

Yield: 1 1/2 cups

Butter Sauce

This is a recipe for a basic butter sauce. I say basic because from here you can adapt it to make many different variations. Try adding fresh herbs, a little minced ginger, roasted red peppers or some tequila and lime. The possibilities are virtually endless.

One important ingredient of this sauce is some form of acidity. I usually use lemon juice. You can also use vinegar, lime juice, some white wine, alcohol (tequila, vodka, etc.), or any combination of any or all. This really depends on what flavor you're going for and what you're serving it with.

The trick to this sauce is temperature. If you get it too hot the butter will separate from the liquid and you have to start over. If you let it get too cool and then try to reheat it, same outcome. If this happens it will mostly be flavored melted butter. This isn't all bad; it just won't have the same smooth texture as the sauce. Just tell your family or whoever you're serving it to that it's what you intended and they can try and make that "fancy" butter sauce sometime if they want.

This sauce is great with fish or seafood.

Ingredients:

2 tablespoons minced shallots (regular onion will also work)
1/4 cup lemon juice*
2 tablespoons heavy cream
8 ounces cold cubed unsalted butter
salt

Place shallots and lemon juice in a heavy sauce pan over medium low heat, bring to simmer and reduce by one half. Add the cream and reduce by half again. This mixture should be slightly thick.

Now comes the tricky part. Turn the heat down to low. With a whisk in one hand and the butter in the other, start to add the butter one cube at a time. Whisk in each cube until it's melted. Once one cube is just about melted add the next and so on until all the butter is incorporated.**

From here you don't want to get it too hot. The best way to tell this is to stick your finger in the sauce (don't tell anyone). If the sauce seems about room temperature, let it get a little more heat. If you see steam coming off of the sauce or little pools of melted butter starting to form on top, it's getting too hot. If that starts to happen, get it out of the pan as soon as you can. Best to put it in a small metal bowl, which will disperse the heat quicker than a plastic container.

Now you can hold the sauce warm for up to several hours until you need to use it. Again, just don't try to reheat it the next day or you'll end up with melted butter.

*This is where you can substitute tequila or wine or any other type of acid.

* *Here's where you can vary it with optional ingredients, like herbs, ginger, red peppers, or whatever.

Yield: 4 two-ounce servings

CHIPOTLE SHELLFISH BROTH

Very early in the life of the restaurant Jane and I went to Santa Fe for a little R&R. One of the restaurants we went to didn't have a lot of sauces on their menu; they used interesting broths instead – ones that are thickened slightly with puréed vegetables. From that experience I started experimenting with some recipes. This is one of my favorites.

The great thing about using broths is they aren't as heavy as most regular sauces. That way you can use a larger potion as opposed to a reduction sauce, and they can be relatively healthy. In this one, the onion and tomato give a little body while the chipotle lends heat and smokiness.

This is a really nice match with seafood. I especially like it with halibut or salmon that has been topped with a Roasted Tomato Gratin (page 117) and served with Mashed Potatoes (page 50). The mashed potatoes and the heat from the broth make for a perfect winter dish.

INGREDIENTS:

2 tablespoons vegetable oil
1 cup chopped tomatoes
1 1/2 cups sliced onions
4 cloves garlic
1 1/2 teaspoons canned chipotle peppers
3 cups shellfish stock*
salt

Heat oil in a heavy pot over medium flame. Add tomatoes, onions and garlic and sauté until they start to wilt – probably about 5 to 10 minutes. Try not to get any color on the veggies as it can affect the color of the finished product. Add chipotle and stock and bring to a boil over high heat. Turn down to low and simmer until the garlic cloves are cooked through and mushy. This should take about 10 to 15 minutes. Purée mixture in a blender and strain through a sieve. This will remove any tomato seeds and skins. Add salt to taste.

*You can use homemade stock, such as Shrimp Stock (page 103). Or bottled clam juice works really well for this. If you use clam juice you probably won't need to add any salt as the juice is pretty salty already.

Yield: 4 cups

Ginger Lemongrass Shellfish Broth

Even though I'm a big fan of intense reduction sauces, I've come to love broths. They can be a great option for subtler flavors that won't fill you up as much as a reduction sauce. This one is really nice with seared sea scallops or shrimp. It can also be used as a base for a simple seafood soup.

The use of store-bought clam juice in this recipe is an easy shortcut. If you happen to have some homemade shrimp stock lying around, feel free to use it. You should be able to find lemongrass at any Asian market and at some farmers' market where Hmong growers sell this and other Southeast Asian specialties. If you can't find lemongrass, fresh lemon juice and zest will suffice. When slicing the lemongrass, start at the fat end and go about three-quarters of the way up the stalk. At this point it will start to get really woody and tough, so you can toss the rest.

Low and slow on the sautéing of the veggies is the way to go here. If they start to brown, the color of your broth won't be as appealing. Remember this is going to be puréed and strained so the cutting of the veggies doesn't have to be pretty. You also won't need much salt if any because the clam juice already contains a fair amount.

Ingredients:

2 tablespoons vegetable oil
2 cups sliced onions
1 stalk sliced lemongrass
4 cloves garlic
3 tablespoons minced ginger root
1 diced Roma tomato
3 cups bottled clam juice

Heat oil in a heavy sauce pan until barely hot. Add next 5 ingredients and turn the heat down to medium low. Stir the veggies once every few minutes until the tomato starts to break apart. Add the clam juice and simmer until the garlic cloves are mushy, about 20 minutes. Purée the broth in a blender until smooth. (An immersion blender won't work as well here because the lemongrass is too fibrous.) Strain through a sieve and make sure to push all the liquid through.

Yield: 3 to 3 1/2 cups

Five Spice Raspberry Barbeque Sauce

The name of this sauce might be misleading. It is pretty intense to be used as an all-purpose barbeque sauce. I like to use it as more of a glaze to finish meats on the grill. It works great with salmon, chicken, and duck. It's also a good dipping sauce for ribs or wings.

The five spice powder that's called for here is becoming pretty commonplace in grocery stores. It can also be found in most Asian markets.

In the restaurant I use seedless raspberry purée. Feel free to use frozen raspberries (about 3/4 cup), although you may have to cook it longer to get the desired consistency. A raspberry flavored liqueur will also work well.

With all of the acidic, salty, and sweet ingredients in this sauce it will keep for many weeks in the refrigerator.

Ingredients:

2 tablespoons sesame oil
2 cloves garlic, minced
1 tablespoon minced ginger root
1/2 cup rice vinegar
juice of 1 lemon
2 tablespoons soy sauce
2 tablespoons tomato paste
2 tablespoons brown sugar
1 tablespoon five spice powder
1/4 cup raspberry purée or 2 tablespoons raspberry liqueur

Place sesame oil in a heavy sauce pan over low heat. Add garlic and ginger and sauté just until they sizzle a little, 1-2 minutes. Add remaining ingredients and whisk until smooth. Simmer for 5 to 10 minutes, stirring frequently. Make sure not to boil this sauce, as it will thicken very quickly.

Yield: 1 1/4 cups

CHILLED CUMIN CREAM

Here's another of those easy cold garnish-type sauces I really like. Use it as a fancy and flavorful garnish on Black Bean and Chorizo Soup (page 23) or with Crawfish Cakes (page 8).

Fresh squeezed lime juice is the way to go with this sauce. I feel the reconstituted doesn't quite cut it, but it will work in a pinch.

INGREDIENTS:

1 cup sour cream
1/4 cup fresh lime juice
1 tablespoon ground cumin
1 teaspoon salt

Whisk all ingredients together until smooth. Refrigerate until ready to use.

Yield: 1 1/4 cups

Garlic Cream Sauce

There are a couple things I like about this sauce. First I really like a sauce that is thickened with its own natural ingredients (in this case, heavy cream and softened garlic) as opposed to an outside thickening agent (like a flour-based roux). The second reason is that with this sauce you get an additional product to use later on: the oil used to cook the garlic.

The cooking of the garlic is the tricky part. You want to make sure that you don't cook it too fast or too long. Either of these can make the garlic bitter and gummy in texture.

One way to cook the garlic is to place the peeled cloves in a heavy sauce pan and cover them in olive oil. Put it over very low heat and just simmer them until the cloves are mushy. If they start to get dark in color then the heat is too high. It should take 35 to 45 minutes. Another way is to roast the garlic in the oven. Place the garlic and the oil in a shallow roasting pan and cover them with foil. Roast in a 250-degree oven for 30 to 40 minutes until the garlic is soft.

Either way you prepare the oil, after it's done you'll have some delicious flavored oil for other uses – dip crusty bread into it or drizzle it on salad greens with some balsamic vinegar.

Serve this sauce with pan-seared salmon – or it would go very nicely with a simple chicken and rice dish.

Ingredients:

1/4 cup peeled garlic cloves
1/2 cup olive oil
1 cup half-and-half
salt and pepper

To cook the garlic: Follow one of the methods described above. Drain the garlic but keep the oil for other uses.

For the sauce: Place the softened garlic and half-and-half in a blender and purée until smooth. Strain through a sieve and add salt and pepper to taste. Heat sauce over low heat. Note: it might thicken slightly when heated; just thin it out with a little water to the desired consistency before serving.

Yield: About 1 to 1 1/4 cups

Ginger Sherry Cream Sauce

There are two different ways to make this sauce, the first being that you can purée and strain the sauce (my personal preference). The other is to mince the onion and ginger and leave them in the sauce to give it a different texture.

This is great with bay scallops over angel hair pasta – the sherry and ginger really compliment the scallops. One thing to be careful of if you serve this sauce with scallops is the liquid that might come out of them when they are cooked. This could thin out the sauce. Make sure to cook the scallops separately before mixing them into the finished sauce.

Ingredients:

2 tablespoons vegetable oil
1/2 cup sliced onion
2 tablespoons minced ginger
1/3 cup dry cooking sherry
2/3 cup shellfish stock (bottled clam juice also works well)
1 1/3 cups heavy cream
1 tablespoon cornstarch or arrowroot
2 tablespoons water

Heat oil over medium low heat in a heavy sauce pan. Cook the onions and ginger for several minutes, stirring occasionally and making sure not to get any color on them – this could turn the sauce a not-so-desirable color. Add the sherry, increase the heat to medium-high and simmer the sauce until it is reduced by half. Add the stock and cream and simmer until the onion is cooked through and soft.

This is the point when you can go either way with the sauce. You can skip to the thickening part of the recipe; otherwise, it's time to get out the heavy machinery. Pour the sauce into a blender, attach the lid and purée well. Watch out so the sauce doesn't splash out of the blender when you turn it on. Strain the sauce through a fine sieve, return it back to the sauce pan and bring to a boil. Mix the cornstarch with the water and dissolve well. While whisking the sauce, pour the cornstarch mixture in and boil the sauce for about 10 seconds.

At this point you might want to add some salt. If you used clam juice be wary as the clam juice can be salty already.

Yield: 2 1/4 cups

Honey Bourbon Barbeque Sauce

The thing about barbeque sauces are that they're like a good batch of chili – always better the next day (if there's any left over). I think it takes that time in the refrigerator for all the flavors to come together and to get that optimal sauce euphoria.

This sauce is real straightforward, with the tanginess coming from the balsamic vinegar and the sweetness coming from the honey and the beer. Unfortunately you may have some beer left over after putting your sauce together, so make wise decisions on how to dispose of it. I suggest drinking it to make sure it's of a high enough quality for the meat or fish that the sauce will accompany.

A few notes: Cheap bourbon is just fine for this recipe; save the good stuff for your own private quality time. You probably won't need much salt, because the ketchup already has some (but as always it's up to the cook's discretion). Also make sure that when you are adding your bourbon to take the sauce pan away from the open flame of the stove so the kitchen doesn't go up in flames.

Ingredients:

2 tablespoons vegetable oil
1/2 cup diced onion
4 cloves garlic, minced
1/2 cup honey
1/2 cup bourbon
1/4 cup balsamic vinegar
1/4 cup dark beer
1 teaspoon chile powder
1 teaspoon dry thyme
3 cups ketchup
salt and pepper to taste

Heat the oil in a heavy sauce pan over a medium flame. Add the onions and garlic and sauté them for several minutes. Add the remaining ingredients and simmer over low heat 30-40 minutes, making sure to stir it every so often.

Yield: About 5 cups

Honey Habañero Barbeque Sauce

This sauce, like the honey bourbon barbeque left, gets its sweetness from honey, but also from some cola. Feel free to use whatever brand you want, just don't use diet. The sweetness will also help to calm the heat of the habañero peppers, although it should still have a fair amount of kick. Although the habañeros give this sauce that good heat, the thing I really like about them is the flavor. The five spice powder also gives it a bit of an Asian feel.

Be sure to wear plastic or latex gloves while working with the habañeros, and don't touch any sensitive parts of yourself (eyes, nose, lips) or you may get quite a burning sensation in that area. If you're worried about not being careful enough with the gloves, you can always rent a Hazmat suit from your local fire department.

This sauce will keep in the refrigerator for many weeks because of the vinegar and sugar content.

Ingredients:

- 2 tablespoons vegetable oil
- 1 1/2 cups diced onion
- 8 cloves garlic, minced
- 2 habañero peppers, seeded and diced
- 3 cups ketchup
- 1 cup honey
- 1 cup cider vinegar
- 1 cup cola
- 1 tablespoon five spice powder
- salt (optional)

Heat oil in a heavy sauce pan over a medium flame. Add the onions and garlic and sauté them for several minutes. Add remaining ingredients and simmer over low heat for about 45 minutes. Add salt to taste if necessary.

Yield: About 6 cups

Mango Ginger Salsa

Sometimes at the restaurant one of our floor staff will set a dish in front of a guest and the diner will say, "This is too beautiful to eat." Well, that's a reaction you might get when you make this salsa. The mango, red pepper and red onion along with the cilantro are like a party in a bowl. Oh, and it also tastes good.

This is a perfect summertime salsa for grilled fish, chicken or pork.
Don't forget the mojitos!

Ingredients:

2 cups diced fresh mango
1/4 cup diced red onion
1/4 cup diced red bell pepper
1 teaspoon minced fresh ginger root
2 tablespoons chopped cilantro
1 tablespoon fresh lime juice
salt to taste

Combine all the ingredients in a bowl and mix well. Use it right away or refrigerate until you're ready. I wouldn't recommend refrigerating too long, as the onions and peppers will start to get soggy.

Yield: 2 1/2 cups

Parmesan Cream Sauce

How can you not like this sauce? It has two of the great culinary buzzwords – cream and Parmesan. This works well with pasta and some grilled shrimp or chicken.

For this sauce you will essentially be making a roux with the oil and flour; it will be the thickening agent for the sauce. The Parmesan will also thicken it slightly at the end.

A couple of things to be watchful of: Make sure when you sauté the garlic that you don't get the oil too hot or the garlic could easily burn. And use some decent Parmesan if you have it available. You're worth it.

Ingredients:

3 tablespoons vegetable oil
1 clove garlic, minced
3 tablespoons flour
2 cups milk
1/2 cup half & half
1/4 pound grated Parmesan
    (about 1 1/2 cups total)
salt

Heat oil in a heavy sauce pan over medium low heat, add garlic, and sauté it for just a minute or two. Whisk in the flour until smooth, and cook for another minute or so until it becomes kind of bubbly.

Slowly add the milk and half & half, whisking constantly. The whisking action is very important to prevent the sauce from turning out lumpy. Once all of the liquid is added bring sauce to a boil – this will ensure that the roux is thickening to its fullest potential. Then turn it down to low and whisk in the cheese until it's melted. Add salt if necessary but know that some cheeses have a higher salt content than others. Make sure to taste the sauce before you add any salt.

Yield: 2 3/4 to 3 cups

Roasted Poblano Cream Sauce

This is one of my very favorite sauces. Even though it is a cream-style sauce it isn't as heavy as some people perceive a cream sauce to be.

The roasting of the poblano peppers is key to the flavor here. The easiest way is to roast them is to have your husband or your wife do it, so you don't have to. If that isn't an option here are two other methods: Lightly coat the peppers with oil or pan spray. Place them directly over a high flame on your gas stove and turn them periodically until the skin is charred black. (If you have an electric stove, throw it out the window and buy a gas range.) Or you can slice the oiled peppers in half lengthwise and place them under a hot broiler until the skin is blistered and partially charred.

Whichever way you do it, know that the peppers don't have to perfectly roasted because this recipe is puréed and strained; thus, any bits of skin or seeds are removed. But make sure not to get any gray spots on the peppers, this means you have roasted them too long and have burned through that spot.

After the peppers are roasted place them in a covered container until they're completely cooled. The skin and the seeds will then come off very easily, especially if they are left in the refrigerator overnight in the covered container.

As for the sauce, it can be made a day ahead and reheated when you are ready to use it. It's awesome with the Cornmeal and Habañero Crusted Pork Cutlets on page 126.

Ingredients:

1 tablespoon vegetable oil
2 large poblano peppers (each about 4-5 ounces when raw), roasted, peeled and seeded
1 diced Roma tomato
1/2 teaspoon ground cumin
1 cup half-and-half
salt to taste

Heat oil in a heavy bottom saucepan until barely hot. Add poblanos and tomato and sauté, stirring occasionally, until the tomatoes start to break down. Add cumin and half-and-half and bring to a boil. As soon as the sauce boils turn the heat down to maintain a low simmer. If you boil the sauce too hard it will reduce too much and can get very thick. Let it simmer for about 10 to 15 minutes.

Purée the sauce until smooth with an immersion blender or your favorite margarita blender. Strain it through a fine sieve, making sure to push all the liquid through. Discard any skin or seeds in the sieve. Season the sauce with salt to taste and thin with a little water if desired.

Yield: 1 1/4 to 1 1/2 cups, or about 4 three-ounce servings.

Sweet Corn Sauce

Here is another example of a sauce that is puréed to thicken it. The corn and the onions are cooked down slowly with the milk and then puréed, for a great sauce that is really versatile. I like to sauce seafood or chicken with it, but it could also be used as a soup if the neighbors show up unexpectedly.

You can use canned or frozen corn, but I prefer to use the fresh-stuff cut right off the cob. Don't worry if you leave a little corn silk or husk on the cobs when you cut the kernels off. These will be strained out when you finish the sauce.

If you really want to make this sauce awesome, try using half-and-half or heavy cream instead of milk. This will, of course, increase the flavor and calories, but will also increase your popularity with the local dairy farmers.

Ingredients:

2 tablespoons vegetable oil
1 1/2 cups sliced onion
2 cups sweet corn kernels (about 3 cobs-worth)
2 1/2 cups milk
salt

Heat oil in a heavy pot over low flame. Sauté onions and corn until the onions start to soften, 10-15 minutes. Add milk and bring to a simmer over medium-low heat. Continue to simmer until onions are soft, another 10-15 minutes. Purée all ingredients in a blender until very smooth. Strain through a sieve and add salt to taste.

Yield: 4 cups

TOMATILLO SALSA

This salsa has fewer ingredients but a little more technique than a straightforward fresh salsa. The charring of the tomatillos and tomatoes might be a little scary for some, but it's very easy. If you are intimidated by the charring process feel free to invite me over and I will be happy to help. Of course I'd expect to stay for dinner and cocktails afterward.

There are several ways to char the tomatillos. The first is in a very hot sauté pan, which is the way I've described it in the instructions below. The other two ways are on your outdoor grill over a hot fire and in the oven under the broiler. Whatever way you char the tomatillos, make sure not to cook them all the way through; otherwise, your salsa won't have that good astringent tomatillo flavor.

All you need is a bag of chips or some tortillas to serve as the vehicle for this wonderful salsa.

INGREDIENTS:

3-4 medium tomatillos (about 1/2 pound total), husks removed
1 Roma tomato
1 tablespoon chopped fresh cilantro
1/2 teaspoon minced canned chipotle pepper
juice of 1/2 lime
salt to taste

To char the tomatillos: Heat a regular (as in not nonstick) sauté pan over high flame for 5-10 minutes. (Make sure that the pan is very clean before starting or you might create a little smoke.) Place the whole tomatillos and tomatoes directly in the pan without any oil. You won't get the entire skin charred, which is okay. You'll get a nice patch of black on each side so to speak. Once they start to give off some liquid, but still hold their shape, remove them from the pan.

From here you can make either a chunky or smooth salsa. For smooth simply place all the ingredients in a blender and purée till you have achieved your desired consistency. For chunky just cut the tomatillos and tomatoes by hand into the size you want and then add the remaining ingredients.

Yield: 1 to 1 1/4 cups

Thai Peanut Sauce

There are some peanut sauces that start with whole peanuts. They have you toast them and grind them and do all sorts of things to them. Well, for this sauce we are going to use one of the greatest inventions ever: peanut butter. Ah, simplicity.

The versatility of this sauce is wonderful. It can be used as a dipping sauce with, for example, the Cornmeal-Crusted Portobella Mushrooms on page 6. You could also thin it out with a little more water and use to baste pork or chicken on the grill.

Make sure when you add the liquid that you add it slowly; otherwise it might seep out the seams of your food processor.

This will keep for several weeks in the refrigerator.

Ingredients:

3/4 cup creamy peanut butter*
juice of 1/2 lime (about 1 tablespoon)
1 tablespoon red Thai curry paste
1/2 cup water
1 tablespoon soy sauce

Place peanut butter, lime juice and curry paste in a food processor. With the motor running slowly add the water and soy sauce until well incorporated. You'll need to scrape the sides and corners of the processor bowl to make sure everything is well combined.

Yield: 1 1/2 cups

* Different brands of peanut butter have different consistencies and sugar contents – just use your favorite creamy type. You could also use chunky if you like. But that's living on the edge.

Smoked Tomato Remoulade

This is a wonderful sauce for most grilled fish, crab cakes, or the Crawfish Cakes on page 8. It is really isn't a traditional remoulade, but you're the cook so you can name it anything you want.

The use of the liquid smoke flavoring is kind of cheating, but it is a natural product and it tastes good. Be careful when measuring it as it's very strong. For the roasted tomatoes, refer to page 116; the roasting concentrates and intensifies the flavor. The remoulade will keep for up to a week or two in the refrigerator.

Ingredients:

2/3 cup lightly packed Oven Roasted Tomatoes
juice of 1/2 lemon
1 1/2 cups mayonnaise
1/4 teaspoon liquid smoke flavoring
salt to taste (if needed)

Combine all ingredients in a food processor and purée until smooth. You might not need any salt. It depends on how salty the tomatoes and mayonnaise are.

Yield: 2 cups

Indian Curry Vinaigrette

As with the Black Bean Vinaigrette (see page 63), this dressing veers from the traditional. I've added sour cream to give it a smoother texture and also make it a little more pleasing to the eye. The sour cream will also keep it from separating so easily.

You can make this with either hot or mild curry powder, whatever you prefer. This is a really refreshing summertime dressing for chilled seafood, or for a recipe like the Chilled Salmon Salad on page 33.

Ingredients:

1/2 cup rice vinegar
1 tablespoon curry powder
1/3 cup sour cream
3/4 cup pure olive oil
salt

Combine all ingredients in a bowl and whisk until smooth. When this is chilled, the oil might solidify a bit and make the consistency a little funky. If that happens just whisk it again until it comes together. The lighter the oil the less chance of that happening.

Yield: 1 3/4 cups

reduction sauces

Chicken Stock
Reduced Chicken Stock

The keys to making a good stock with a good yield are the amount of water you have in your stock pot, and patience. Too little water doesn't give you a good yield, and you don't want your bones too crowded in the pot – you want to be able to stir them, and make sure they are covered with liquid at all times. Too much water makes a less rich, watery stock.

You need patience because making chicken stock can be a several-day process from beginning to end. For instance, at the restaurant I start with thirty pounds of bones and about twelve gallons of water, which yields about three-quarters of a gallon of reduced stock. (A side note here: I call it reduced stock, while others call it those fancy French terms like demi-glace, or just demi or glace). I roast the bones and vegetables one day, make and strain the stock the next day. On the third day I reduce the stock… and on the fourth day he rested.

There are a couple of ways you can go about getting chicken bones for stock. The first way is to buy whole chickens and butcher them yourself; that is, remove the breast, leg, and thigh meat to use for another dish (a four-pound bird will yield about a 2 to 2 1/2 pound carcass). The other way is to roast the birds whole and then remove the meat. If you roast them whole you won't need to roast the bones again, however you may not get as good of a yield of stock as you do when you start with raw bones.

Also, if you roast whole birds, don't forget to remove the giblet bag from inside the bird; otherwise you may get liver-flavored stock.

Ingredients:

4 pounds chicken bones
2 ribs diced celery
2 diced onions
3 diced carrots

2 sprigs fresh parsley
4 sprigs fresh thyme
2 bay leaves
6 peppercorns
water

Roast bones, celery, onions, and carrots on a large roasting pan in a preheated 400-degree oven until bones are starting to brown and vegetables are getting some good color on them, about 45 minutes. Some parts of the veggies might even be slightly burned, which is just fine.

Place bones, veggies, and remaining ingredients in a heavy-bottomed 16-quart stock pot, covering the ingredients with enough water to reach just a few inches from the top of the pot. You rarely can have too much water, but if you have too little it will affect your yield.

Take a little water and put it in the roasting pan and scrape all the stuff that was stuck to the pan until you get all or most of it. Add the water with the scrapings in it to your stock pot. Bring the stock to a boil over high heat and then turn it down to a simmer right away. Simmer for 4 to 5 hours, adding additional water if too much is evaporating (that is, if the liquid level starts to go below the level of the bones).

When the stock is done, strain out the solids. Let the stock sit for a few minutes or longer so that the fat layer rises to the top. Remove the fat layer – this can be done with a ladle, and then you can gently lay some pieces of paper towel on top one at a time to get that last thin layer of fat. You can also chill the stock overnight and just peel the solidified fat layer off the next day.

At this point you have "regular" chicken stock, which can be used to make soups or anything that requires a broth. For a reduced stock, there's one more step. This part is as easy as boiling water, which is what you are essentially doing. Make sure you do this in a heavy-bottomed stock pot, to reduce the risk of scorching the stock if it boils down too far. Just boil the stock over high heat until it gets quite a bit darker and visibly thicker. When the stock is fully reduced, the bubbles will also get bigger and will sustain their shape for longer time. When a reduced stock is cooled it should hold its shape very well and should be dark brown in color.

Yield: About 1 to 1 1/2 gallons chicken stock, or about 2 to 2 1/2 cups reduced chicken stock

Maple Bourbon Mustard Sauce

Here is another reduction-style sauce that uses the Reduced Chicken Stock on page 90. The bourbon, mustard and maple syrup work really well together to give it that sweet and savory flavor, while the stock and cream help to thicken it and balance all the flavors.

This is a real hit at the restaurant when served with the Spice Rubbed Pork Tenderloin on page 126.

I like to use a really coarse-ground mustard in the sauce. The coarser types just seem to be less acidic, but feel free to use your favorite style. The type of bourbon probably isn't that crucial, as there are a lot of other flavors going on (so save the good stuff for your own special quality time). Do be careful when heating the bourbon so your kitchen doesn't go up in flames. Don't let it come in contact with the burner flame or boil too hard by itself in the pan. Isn't cooking exciting?

Ingredients:

1/2 cup bourbon
1/4 cup maple syrup
1/3 cup coarse-ground mustard
2/3 cup heavy cream
1 cup Reduced Chicken Stock

Pour bourbon in a tall-sided heavy sauce pan. This will reduce the risk of the bourbon starting on fire, should some come in contact with the flame. Place over low heat and reduce by about half. It shouldn't take very long to reduce, just a few minutes. If by chance the bourbon catches fire, simply place a lid over it and turn off the heat.

Add remaining ingredients and simmer over medium heat until slightly thickened, about 10 to 15 minutes. Make sure to stir it once in a while as the mustard tends to sink to the bottom of the pan.

Yield: 2 1/2 cups

Port Peppercorn Reduction Sauce

I hope these reduction sauces are starting to make sense to you. Once you have your reduced stock it's a matter of playing with a few other ingredients. This sauce is great with roasted duck.

The reduction of the Port will help to intensify that aspect of this sauce. No need to use anything too expensive, unless it was a gift from a former boss you might not have cared for.

It might seem like there's quite a lot of peppercorns in this recipe. Simmering them in the Port will calm them down a bit. If you choose to swirl in a few chunks of cold butter at the end that will also help. Make sure not to grind the peppercorns too fine or they will overwhelm the other flavors.

There are a couple ways to crush the peppercorns. Using a mortar and pestle is one way. The other is to place them in a metal pie tin and crush them with the back of a small sauté pan. Again, make sure to leave them very coarse.

Ingredients:

1 teaspoon whole black peppercorns. Very coarsely ground
1/2 cup Port wine
1 cup Reduced Chicken Stock (page 90)
4 tablespoons cold cubed butter
salt

Place peppercorns and Port in a heavy sauce pan. Reduce by one-half over low heat. Add stock and continue to simmer for 5 to 10 minutes. Swirl in the butter until just melted and add salt to taste.

Yield: 1 cup

Red Wine Horseradish Reduction Sauce

Even though this sauce has what seems to be like a lot of horseradish in it, it turns out to be quite mild – without the sharpness of the horseradish, just the flavor. This is a great sauce with grilled meats or sausage.

Don't use very high heat when reducing the wine as it is a pretty small amount and you don't want to burn it. Feel free to add a little extra wine if you prefer. Also make sure not to use a wine that is too pricey, and definitely one that isn't too sweet. A Cabernet or Pinot Noir will work really well.

The butter at the end is optional. It will help to give the sauce a bit of a smoother flavor overall. If you do add the butter, make sure not to boil the sauce too much after it is melted or your the butter could separate from the sauce.

Ingredients:

1/3 cup red wine
2 tablespoons prepared horseradish
1/2 cup Reduced Chicken Stock (page 90)
2 tablespoons cold butter
salt and pepper

Place wine in a small heavy sauce pan over medium flame. Simmer briskly until wine is reduced by half. Add horseradish and stock and simmer for about 5 minutes longer, making sure the sauce doesn't get too thick and sticky. Whisk in the butter until just melted and boil for 20 to 30 seconds. Add salt and pepper to taste. You probably won't need much salt as the horseradish may have enough.

Yield: 3/4 cup

Red Wine Truffle Reduction Sauce

Here's a sauce that might be a little decadent – what with the use of truffle – but it's worth it.

There are several ways to buy truffles. The cheapest is probably canned truffle shavings. (They'll come packed in liquid that might have some flavor, but it's probably not worth saving.) Truffle shavings that are left over from this recipe freeze really well for future use. Truffles can also be purchased fresh, but mostly by mail order and at a very steep price. The last way is dried; these just need to be reconstituted in some water overnight. Truffle oil can be found in most specialty-style food stores, and is usually olive oil that has been infused with truffles.

Since most of the cost of this sauce is tied up in the truffles, don't go too overboard on the wine. This is awesome with a nice beef tenderloin.

Note: With the addition of the butter this sauce is best used right after it's made. If you are going to make it ahead and reheat it, add the butter at that time.

Ingredients:

1 cup red wine
1 1/2 teaspoons minced truffle
1 teaspoon truffle oil
1 cup Reduced Chicken Stock (page 90)
4 tablespoons cold butter
salt and pepper

Pour wine in a heavy sauce pan and reduce over medium heat by half. Add truffles, oil and stock and simmer over low heat 5-10 minutes. Whisk in the butter until just melted and remove from heat. Add salt and pepper to taste.

Yield: 1 3/4 cups or enough for about 8 servings

Roasted Tomato Reduction Sauce

Here is a really nice complement to the Oven Roasted Tomatoes on page 116. The little bit of acidity and caramelization adds great depth to this sauce. It's a pretty versatile one that can be used with poultry, pork or beef.

Ingredients:

1/2 cup Oven Roasted Tomatoes
1 cup Reduced Chicken Stock (page 90)
4 tablespoons cubed cold butter
salt and pepper

Simmer tomatoes and stock in a heavy sauce pan over low heat for 5-7 minutes. Purée in a blender* or with an emersion blender until smooth. Strain through a sieve to remove any tomato seeds or skin. Return to the sauce pan and bring back to a simmer over medium heat. Whisk in the butter until just melted. Remove from heat and add salt and pepper to taste.

Yield: 1 1/2 to 1 3/4 cups, or enough for 6 to 8 servings

* Some blender pitchers are designed with ridges so it's hard to scrape out all of the contents. Feel free to drizzle a little water down the sides to rinse out the rest of the sauce. This shouldn't be enough to make the sauce too thin. If you think it is too thin, just reduce it a bit more over low heat.

Vermouth Mustard Sauce

Although this isn't a straight-out reduction sauce, it uses reduced stock in the recipe. The stock, cream and mustard give it body without needing additional thickener, so it's like a reduction sauce. To me this sauce says "Fall or Winter food." It's great paired with roast chicken or turkey around the holidays.

I didn't list salt in the ingredients, mostly because the mustard should have enough to take care of that. Make sure to stir the sauce periodically as the mustard may tend to settle to the bottom of the pan.

And as luck would have it, the recipe will likely leave you with extra vermouth – for those all important martinis when the family comes to visit.

Ingredients:

1 tablespoon vegetable oil
2 shallots, minced
1/3 cup vermouth
1/2 cup Reduced Chicken Stock (page 90)
1/3 cup coarse-ground brown mustard
1/2 cup heavy cream

Heat oil in a small saucepan over medium-low flame. Add shallots and cook for about 1 minute. Add vermouth and reduce liquid by half. Add remaining ingredients and simmer 15-20 minutes.

Yield: 1 1/2 cups

Cherry Reduction Sauce

This is a sauce that some say you could drink by the cupful; however I don't recommend that. I serve this with roasted pork tenderloin, garnished with tart cherries and toasted walnuts. Definitely a house favorite.

In this sauce not only do I use Reduced Chicken Stock, but also reduced cherry juice. You can find cherry juice in the juice aisle of your local store. It usually is unsweetened, but sometimes might have a little sugar added. Make sure it is pure cherry juice, not a juice drink, and for sure not maraschino cherry juice.

The sweetness of the cherry juice and the deep, savory flavor of the stock and cream really work well together. Although it may seem like a lot of cream, it turns out to be a rich, dark-colored pot of deliciousness.

Ingredients:

1 quart cherry juice
1 cup heavy cream
1/4 cup Reduced Chicken Stock (page 90)
3 tablespoons cold cubed butter
salt

Reduce the cherry juice in a heavy pot over high heat, down to 1 cup. Add cream and reduced chicken stock; simmer until slightly reduced and thickened, about 15 minutes. Whisk in the butter until just melted. Remove sauce from heat and add salt to taste. If you are making this a day ahead and reheating it, don't add the butter until you reheat it.

Yield: About 2 cups

White Wine Lemon Caper Reduction Sauce

This is a sauce I serve with sautéed veal cutlets, but also works well with pork or chicken.

It might seem like there is quite a bit of lemon juice in this recipe, but the addition of the butter calms the tartness.

Ingredients:

1/4 cup lemon juice
3/4 cup dry white wine
1 cup Reduced Chicken Stock (page 90)
3 tablespoons cold cubed butter
1/4 cup capers
pepper

Combine lemon juice and wine in a heavy sauce pan. Reduce by one-half over medium heat. This should only take about 5 to 7 minutes. Add stock and simmer 3 to 5 minutes. Whisk in the butter until just melted. Add the capers. Add pepper to taste. The capers have enough salt in them so you shouldn't need to add any additional salt.

Yield: 1 1/2 cups

Horseradish Cider Cream Sauce

This sauce is a combination of reducing two different liquids to thicken it. The apple cider is already reduced when added and will give it the sweetness. The cream will reduce as the sauce is cooking and will give it a savory quality.

It might look like there is quite a bit of horseradish in this sauce and that the flavor could be pretty strong. The truth of it is that the cream and apple cider really kind of calm down and mellow the sharpness, while still letting the flavor come through. Heating it up also tames the horseradish. This works really well with any cut of pork, and the sauce is super simple.

Ingredients:

1 1/2 cups heavy cream
3 tablespoons prepared horseradish (the kind in the jar)
1/3 cup reduced apple cider*
salt and pepper

Combine cream, horseradish and cider in a medium sized heavy sauce pan. The sauce might rise as it cooks so a little larger pan might keep the mess down. Bring to a boil over high heat and reduce to a simmer, stirring occasionally, over low heat. Simmer for 5 to 10 minutes until slightly thickened. Add salt and pepper to taste.

Yield: 1 1/4 cups

*See the info about reducing apple cider on the next page.

Apple Cider Brandy Reduction Sauce

This sauce starts with a reduction of apple cider. Make sure you use a heavy stock pot, to prevent scorching, and one that that is fairly deep – this will help prevent the cider from boiling over the side.

An optional way to finish this sauce is to swirl a few tablespoons of cold butter into the hot sauce when it's ready to serve. This will kind of mellow the sweetness of the cider and the tartness of the vinegar. The flavors remind me of a grown up version of German potato salad. I really like this sauce with sea scallops and even a little crisp bacon added to give it a little smokiness.

You'll end up with some extra reduced cider with this recipe; it will keep in the refrigerator for many months because of the high sugar content. The reduced cider alone is also great over ice cream. Just think how healthy ice cream can be with all that apple juice over it – it's like getting your whole day's worth of fruit in one serving.

Ingredients:

1/2 gallon (8 cups) apple cider
1 tablespoon vegetable oil
1 cup diced onion
1/4 cup brandy
1/3 cup apple cider vinegar
salt and pepper
cold butter (optional)

Bring apple cider to a boil in a heavy pot over a high flame. Let it reduce, without stirring, to 2 cups. Set aside 1/2 cup for the sauce; cool and refrigerate the rest for future use.

Place oil in a heavy sauce pan over medium heat. When oil is hot, add the onion and saute for several minutes until onion is almost cooked through. It's okay if the onion gets a little color on it. Add the brandy* and cider vinegar and simmer over low heat for about 15 minutes. Don't worry about the sauce reducing too much; that will just intensify the flavor. Add salt and pepper to taste. If you are going to finish it with butter, now is the time. Just swirl in a few tablespoons until the butter is just melted.

*Remember to add the brandy away from the open flame of the stove, unless you're trying to impress your date, then go for it.

Shrimp Stock

Here's another stock you can make besides chicken stock. However, unlike chicken stock, shrimp stock isn't really the best type to reduce too much, as it can tend to get bitter. This stock is great for soups, stews, étouffée, or any other seafood sauce application.

With this recipe, you might find yourself saying, "Where am I going to get shrimp shells?" The best way is when you buy shrimp, buy them with the shells on. Then it comes time to clean them, just freeze the shells until you've accumulated enough to make a batch of stock. They freeze best in a plastic bag with as much air squeezed out of it as possible.

Ingredients:

1/4 cup vegetable oil
1 1/2 pounds shrimp shells (about 8 lightly packed cups)
1 carrot, chopped
1 rib celery, chopped
1 onion, chopped
3 chopped Roma tomatoes
1 tablespoon chopped fresh thyme
1/2 cup brandy
6 cloves garlic

Heat oil in a heavy stock pot over medium high heat. Add shrimp shells and sauté them until they start to get some color. Add carrot, celery and onion and sauté for several more minutes. Add the tomatoes and continue to sauté until the bottom of the pot starts to accumulate some good brown color, but not anything darker.

 Add the brandy and deglaze the pot – that means stir up all the brown goodness that's sticking to the bottom of the pot. When all the brown goodness is released, add the garlic and 2 gallons water. Bring the mixture to a boil.

Turn heat down to produce a low simmer and cook the stock 1 1/2 to 2 hours. Strain the stock and discard all of the solids. Cool the stock and remove any fat that has solidified on top. There probably won't be that much.

From here you can reduce it (read: boil it down) by about half to intensify the flavor, or just leave it as is.

Yield: 1 1/4 to 1 1/2 gallons, depending on how much it has reduced.

Our Kids

Early in our relationship, Jane and I decided that we didn't want to have children. A few years after starting the restaurant, we realized that we didn't have a choice.

We employ quite a few kids of high school age, and in a small town there aren't a whole lot of activities for them to do. When we hire them they usually let us know that they will have to quit when they go off to college. For anyone in the restaurant business, getting a three-year notice is pretty nice. And working with them for three years means there's going to be some sort of relationship formed. Because of this we've realized that we actually have some influence on these young minds.

We get to teach them life lessons like, "Be polite to your parents," "Say please and thank you," "A clean kitchen is a happy kitchen," and "Fire is your friend."

When our first ones left for college we often hired their younger siblings to replace them. This started a trend and we have done that with quite a few families in the area. One father thanked us for the fact that he knew where his daughter was every Saturday night.

I think we started realizing that we really did have kids when they started coming back just to say hi, and to tell us what was going on in their lives. Soon they were having their wedding dinners at the restaurant, coming in to show us their first-born, and stopping in to give us a hug when they were home from the Gulf War.

It's nice to know that even though we're old enough to be their parents we can be friends, too – whether it's going golfing, having them over for a Packer game, or letting them tell us something they would never tell their parents.

The teenage years can be complicated, what with hormones, texting, hair, who likes who, and like, OMG, did you friend me on Facebook? Well, at least I didn't have to change any diapers.

Go-Alongs

I've always been a fan of interesting accompaniments that go along with entrées, appetizers, soups or salads. Whether it's a glaze, a relish, a chutney or caramelized onions, go-alongs are little additions that can really take a dish to another level.

Some of the preparations in this section can be used in sauces or as toppings for meat or fish. Others, such as the cranberry chutney, might be good with cheese or on a roast beef sandwich. Or you can use them as part of an appetizer platter.

However you use them, have fun, experiment and enjoy!

go-alongs

Caramelized Onions

So you read this recipe and you say to yourself "What the heck am I going to do with all of these caramelized onions?" Don't worry, we'll get there.

One of the key ingredients for this process is patience. This is going to take time, attention, a spoon, and a heavy pot. The heavy pot is important so that the onions don't burn.

So what about these onions I speak of? Well, when an onion is fresh it can be quite strong in flavor and in scent. We're going to slowly cook the onions over low heat to get rid of the strong flavor and bring out the natural sugars. That's what caramelizing does.

The uses for them are countless – from soups to relishes to toppings for fish. One of my favorites is to use them in place of sauce on a pizza. If you have extra, they freeze very well, too.

Now let's get to caramelizing…

Ingredients:

1/4 cup vegetable oil
3 pounds sliced sweet onions (such as Vidalia or Walla Walla)
salt

Place oil in a heavy pot over high heat and when the oil is fairly hot, add the onions. Stir the onions every so often until you start to see some color on them, about 15 minutes. Now you want to turn your heat down to about medium. What you don't want to see is really dark color a.k.a. burning. If you see that, turn your heat down lower. Continue to stir the onions every once in a while. They should start to turn a golden caramel color as they start to break down and become soft. This should take 45 minutes to an hour. They will really cook down in volume quite a bit. Once they become a mass of golden and almost sticky deliciousness, they are ready to salt to taste.

Now go forth and create something yummy.

Yield: 2 cups

Carmelized Onion and Bacon Relish

This is a one of my favorite little go-alongs, a relish we usually use to complement the Spice Rubbed Pork Tenderloin (p. 126) and the Maple Bourbon Mustard Sauce (p. 92). It also goes well with grilled steak or other cuts of pork.

The flavors in this remind me of German-style potato salad. You have the sweetness of the Caramelized Onions (p. 108), the smokiness of the bacon, and the tanginess of the cider vinegar.

The bacon can be done one of two ways. The first – and the way I like to do it – is to chop the bacon, then cook it in a heavy sauté pan over medium-low heat until most of the fat is rendered out and the bacon is still a touch chewy. If you like your bacon a little crispier just go a little longer. This will take about 20 to 30 minutes. The fat will start to get kind of foamy when the bacon is close to being done.

The second way is to cook the bacon slices whole, the way you would for breakfast. Then chop or crumble them into desired size pieces. Either way you do it you can't go wrong. It's bacon.

Ingredients:

- 1 1/2 cups chopped and cooked bacon with the fat drained off (this is about 1 pound raw)
- 3/4 cup Caramelized Onions
- 2 tablespoons apple cider vinegar
- 1/4 teaspoon black pepper

Mix all the ingredients together and refrigerate until needed. When you do need it you can just warm it in the oven for a few minutes. Then top your pork or steak with a good dollop.

This will also freeze very well.

Yield: About 1 3/4 cup – enough for 8 to 12 portions, depending on their size.

cranberry chutney

The thing I love most about chutney is its versatility – how you can interchange different ingredients. For example, you could take this recipe and replace the raisins with dates or figs and come out with a different version. I also love the sweet and sour aspect of chutney. This is a great one to use with a chilled meat appetizer – such as prosciutto, which would add a great salty contrast to the sweet-tart chutney. And this would be wonderful on a roast beef sandwich. It will keep for several weeks in the refrigerator because the sugar and vinegar help preserve it.

ingredients:

1 1/2 cups fresh or frozen cranberries
2 tablespoons balsamic vinegar
1/2 cup raisins
1/2 teaspoon ground coriander
salt to taste (optional)

Combine all ingredients except salt in a heavy sauce pan and cook over low heat until cranberries start to disintegrate and turn mushy. Add salt to taste, if desired, and chill.

Yield: 3/4 to 1 cup

Honey Citrus Glaze

This is a super simple glaze for grilled chicken, fish or shrimp. It works well for sautéed or broiled meats, too; however I like it best on the grilled foods. The sugar in the honey gives a nice dark, caramelized – not to be confused with burned – finish to the meat that really adds additional texture and flavor.

The tartness of the citrus and the sweetness of the honey really complement each other. I prefer to use fresh squeezed citrus juice – that way if you have any left over you can make margaritas or mojitos to go with your meal.

Ingredients:

1 cup honey
2 tablespoons lemon juice
1/4 cup lime juice
2 tablespoons orange juice

Mix all ingredients together and brush on grilled meat or fish during the grilling process. You might want to add a little salt to the glaze. It depends on your own personal taste.

Yield: 1 1/2 cups

Roasted Pickled Garlic

My style of cuisine is constantly evolving. I'm always learning about some new ingredient or technique. Still, one thing that has become a constant is the inclusion of little accompaniments or go-alongs with a meal. Mostly they complete the appearance of the final plating of the food, but they may also add some contrast or brightness to its flavor, or bring another texture to the dish. Roasted pickled garlic does all three.

Roasting the garlic – actually, you're really simmering it in oil – mellows its sharpness, and the pickling preserves it for many weeks. Pickling also adds acidic brightness to the flavor of the dish you're accenting.

As I have explained in earlier recipes, the pan roasting process is the important part. Too-high heat will make the garlic firm, bitter and sticky. The longer and slower it cooks, the easier it is to achieve successful garlic – soft, sweet and smooth.

It may seem like the recipe makes a lot of garlic, but it will keep refrigerated for many weeks. It's great on an antipasto platter or as a companion for soft cheeses.

Note: Some stores sell already peeled garlic. If you can't find that, invite some friends over to help and at least you'll all smell like garlic together.

Ingredients:

2 cups peeled garlic cloves
1 1/3 cups olive oil
1 cup rice vinegar
2 teaspoons dried thyme
1 teaspoon whole peppercorns
2 bay leaves

Place garlic and oil in a heavy sauce pan. Simmer over low heat until garlic is soft. This should take about 30 to 40 minutes. If the garlic starts to turn dark in color, your heat is too high.

Drain the oil from the garlic (store the oil in the refrigerator for future uses) and place garlic in a glass jar or plastic container. Using the same sauce pan, combine remaining ingredients. Bring to a boil and remove from heat. Pour vinegar mixture over garlic. Let this completely cool before covering tightly and refrigerating it. The garlic is ready to eat after sitting overnight.

ginger chimichurri

The addition of ginger to this classic South American condiment gives it a little Asian flavor, with not so much Argentina. This recipe was developed by sous chef Jimmy Sandlin to go along with our Shrimp Cakes appetizer on page 12. It's also fantastic with any grilled fish or seafood, or on turkey sandwiches (that's how my wife eats it).

There are two different ways to prepare this. You can do the more traditional way and chop everything by hand, or you can purée it all in a blender or food processor. If you do it by hand it will be a little chunkier and more like a loose vinaigrette. When you purée it (that's the way I like it) it will be more of a creamy sauce.

ingredients:

1 small shallot, minced
3 cloves garlic, minced
1 tablespoon minced ginger root
packed 1/4 cup chopped parsley
packed 1/4 cup chopped cilantro
1/4 cup rice vinegar
1/2 cup pure olive oil
salt and pepper

Whisk all ingredients except salt and pepper together until well combined. You can also skip the mincing and chopping and just purée the ingredients in a blender or food processor. Add salt and pepper to taste. Chill any unused portion.

Yield: about 1 1/4 cups

MINT CHIPOTLE PESTO

As I've mentioned in other recipes, it's fun to put your own twist on some classics. When I originally developed this pesto, it was used with rack of lamb – thus the mint. I added a bit of a Southwestern feel with the use of chipotle. (The sugar and lemon juice will help to curb the heat of the chipotle, and also give it a longer shelf life.) Pepitas, in case you didn't know, are unsalted raw pumpkin seeds; they're usually found in the bulk foods section of the grocery store. To toast them, place the seeds in a small sauté pan over low heat in just a touch of oil and let them cook until they start to expand and make a popping noise. (The danger level on this procedure is very low.)

It's best to make this pesto a day ahead so the flavors can all get to know each other. Besides going well with rack of lamb, it would also work well with chicken and pork.

INGREDIENTS:

1/2 cup packed fresh mint
1/2 tablespoon canned chipotle pepper
2 cloves garlic
1 1/2 tablespoons lightly toasted pepitas
1/2 teaspoon sugar
1 teaspoon lemon juice
1/4 cup pure olive oil
salt

Purée all ingredients except salt in a food processor until smooth. Add salt to taste and refrigerate.

Yield: about 3/4 cup

Oven Roasted Tomatoes

This is a great way to take some of those underripe tomatoes you might find in the winter – or the summer, for that matter – and concentrate the flavor, for use in quite a few different ways. I've used them on antipasto platters, in reduction sauces, as toppings for fish, as part of vegetable side dishes, in remoulade sauce, or to make a simple vinaigrette.

The key here is to roast them just long enough to hold their shape well without being too mushy or too crispy. You want them to get some good "color" around the edges without burning them completely. Roasting time may vary depending on how thick or thin you slice the tomatoes. Another great thing about these is they will freeze very well.

Ingredients:

2 pounds Roma tomatoes sliced into 1/2 inch rounds
1/2 cup balsamic vinegar
1/4 cup extra virgin olive oil
1 teaspoon salt
1/4 teaspoon black pepper

Heat oven to 350 degrees. Combine all the ingredients and lay in a single layer on a 12-by-18 sheet pan. (You can oil the pan or not – it won't make much of a difference. The oil mixed with the tomatoes will help to keep most of them from sticking.) Roast in oven for about 1 1/2 to 1 3/4 hours, turning the sheet pan every half hour.

Yield: 1 1/2 to 1 3/4 cups

Roasted Tomato Gratin

This is a pretty easy and elegant way to finish off fish, or even a nice steak. The two main ingredients are roasted tomatoes and caramelized onions. If you have those available, you're just a few steps away from success.

Ingredients:

1/2 cup Oven Roasted Tomatoes (previous page)
1/2 cup Caramelized Onions (page 108)
1 tablespoon chopped fresh basil
bread crumbs or grated Parmesan

Combine the tomatoes, onions and basil in a bowl and mix until just combined. I don't like to over mix this. You should be able to distinguish the tomatoes from the onions.

From here you are ready to top your fish or steak. In the last few minutes of cooking – whether it's in the oven or on the grill – spread about 2 tablespoons of gratin on top of your future meal. Then sprinkle it with either bread crumbs or Parmesan. Place it back into the oven or grill and let the crumbs just get brown and the gratin get hot.

Yield: 1 cup, or about 6 to 8 servings

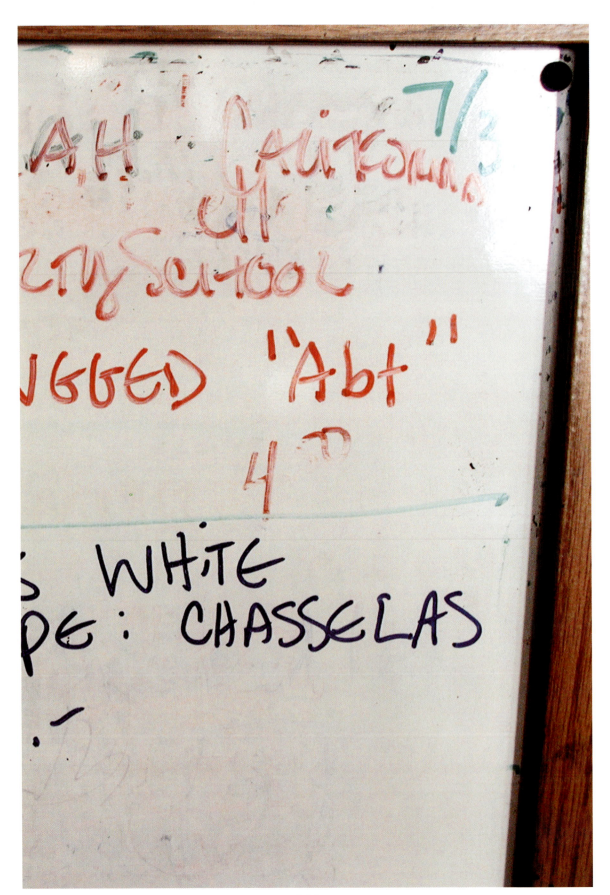

Two Olive Caper Relish

The saltiness of the olives and capers and the smoothness of the olive oil make this a great relish to partner with grilled fish. You can always substitute your favorite type of olives for the ones below, and for you garlic lovers, feel free to double the garlic. This is best if it sits awhile to let the flavors come together, but can definitely be used right away.

Some preparation advice to go with this recipe: Remove the pimentos before quartering them. Don't bother pitting the Kalamatas yourself; you can buy them already pitted. To seed the tomato, cut it into quarters lengthwise, then lay each quarter skin side down on the cutting board and run your knife between the seeds and the outer meat of the tomato.

Ingredients:

1/2 cup quartered green olives
1/2 cup pitted and quartered Kalamata olives
1 large seeded and diced Roma tomato
1 small garlic clove, minced
2 tablespoons capers
2 tablespoons extra virgin olive oil

Combine all ingredients. Use right away or refrigerate for future use.

Yield: 1 1/2 cups

Jane and Her Wine

Here at the restaurant we have quite an extensive, and award winning wine list, usually around 140 to 150 different wines. Small compared to some lists and large to others. Well I think it's pretty extensive anyway. Jane is the wine guru, and can tell you about any wine on the list.

Some people think "what a great job, you get to go to wine tastings for free and just drink wine". Well it's not that easy of a job. Try tasting 60 different wines and then trying to decide which ones will fit the needs for your list. It's quite an art.

Sometimes at the end of the night when things are winding down Jane is nowhere to be found. I've realized over the years that she is usually in the basement petting her precious wine. She really does love it and is very good at what she does. I just hope she doesn't start giving her wine better Christmas gifts than she gives me.

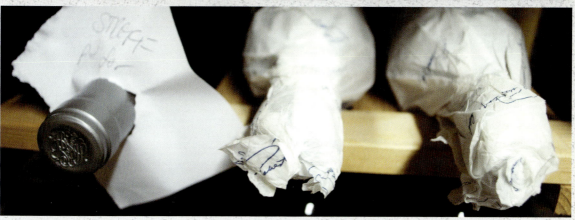

Main Entrées

Herein are some of our favorite main dishes. Some have been featured on the restaurant's menu while others came about in our cooking classes. With some of these recipes I've included suggestions for sauces and sides, too. Here's to the main event!

main entrées

Blue Cheese and Walnut-Stuffed Chicken Breasts

Blue cheese is one of those you-like-it-or-you-don't foods. I like it. I also like butter, so why not combine them? It might look like quite a bit of butter in this case, but it's worth it. One more thing I like: boneless skin-on chicken breasts. The skin gets crispy, which not only adds good color to the chicken, but additional flavor.

Now comes the tricky part: the stuffing of the chicken. There are a couple different ways to make sure that the stuffed breasts look good. One easy way is to use a meat hammer to pound the meat to a uniform thickness and then just form the meat around the stuffing. The second way, and the one I prefer, is to try and get the breasts the same diameter from one end to the other because that way when you slice the meat it looks real showy. To do this, lay the chicken on a cutting board with the skin side down. Use a fillet knife and starting at the center of the breast with the knife almost parallel to the cutting board, slice horizontally towards the right outer edge and through the meat almost to the outside edge (but not all the way!). This will give you a flap of meat that will open up. Now repeat that step with the other side. The chicken should look like you are opening up a book. (Wow, I usually don't get this in-depth about chicken.)

Now on to the recipe.

Ingredients:

1 to 1 1/4 cups crumbed blue cheese (5 ounces)
4 tablespoons diced cold butter
1/2 cup small walnut pieces
1/4 cup bread crumbs
1/4 teaspoon black pepper
4 (six ounces each) boneless skin-on chicken breasts,
   filleted as described at left
olive oil

Combine cheese, butter, walnuts, crumbs and pepper. The best way is to just get in there with your hands, but make sure not to get it too well-combined. It's nice to get a little pocket of butter here and there.

Now place the filleted chicken breasts skin side down on your cutting board. Take four equal amounts of the filling and form each portion into a log that is ½ to 1 inch in diameter and just about the length of the breast. Place one portion of the filling in each piece of chicken. Roll the chicken around the filling and secure with toothpicks. The ends of the chicken breasts sometimes seem to stray. Tuck those in first before you roll it. (These will hold together better if you stuff and then chill them several hours ahead of time.)

To cook the chicken: Heat oven to 425 degrees. Place the stuffed breasts on an oiled baking sheet. Brush or spray the skin with a little olive oil. (This will help the skin get crisp.) Bake about 25 minutes. Remove from the oven and let them sit for a few minutes. Slice on an angle so you can fan the meat out nicely and impress your family. This goes really well with the Sweet Corn Sauce on page 82.

Yield: 4 servings

Cornmeal and Habañero Crusted Pork Cutlets

I think of this as Southwestern schnitzel. The coarseness of the cornmeal and the panko crumbs really give it a crispy texture. If you don't have habañero powder available, use cayenne or any other favorite ground chile pepper. I serve this at the restaurant with the Roasted Poblano Cream Sauce on page 80 and the Cheddar Grits on page 57. Or slap one of these on a bun with some simple slaw and you've got a sandwich that will make your mouth send you flowers.

I call the cooking method here sautéing, but in essence you are really frying the cutlets. Sautéing sounds healthier than frying, so we'll go with that. Remember these will soak up a fair amount of oil, so start with a little and you can always add more as they cook. Just be sure that your pan is fairly hot when you start or your pork could be soggy, not crispy.

If you are going to sauté all eight slices at once you'll need two 12-inch sauté pans. Or you can do them two batches in one pan and hold the first batch in a warm oven while you cook the second.

For the cornmeal dredge:

1 cup coarse-ground cornmeal
1 cup panko crumbs (Japanese style bread crumbs)
2 teaspoons dried oregano
1 teaspoon ground cumin
1 teaspoon kosher salt
1/4 teaspoon habañero powder
2 teaspoons cornstarch

For the pork:

8 slices (each 3 ounces) pork loin, pounded flat
1 egg, beaten
peanut or vegetable oil for sautéing

Mix all cornmeal dredge ingredients together.

Mix pork and egg together so that the pork is well coated. Lay pork in the dredge one cutlet at a time. Put a handful of dredge on top of the pork and press it in firmly so that it will have a nice coat of breading on each side. Repeat until all the pork is breaded.

Add oil to a pretty hot sauté pan and lay the cutlets in the oil, making sure not to let them overlap. Add more oil if it all gets absorbed. Don't be afraid to have some oil left over in the pan when you are done.

Sauté the pork on both sides turning only once, for about 1 1/2 to 2 minutes per side. You want the breading to be a slight golden brown color, but not getting any dark spots. Repeat until all the pork is cooked and then enjoy.

Yield: 4 entrée-size servings or 8 sandwich servings

CHIPOTLE-BRAISED BEEF SHORT RIBS

The cool thing about boneless beef short ribs is that they are like little individual pot roasts – fork-tender and deeply delicious.

You can flavor them how you want. These are flavored with orange juice and chipotle peppers. (In case you haven't noticed, I do have an affinity for chipotles. I use these same flavorings for the Roasted Vegetable Taco Filling on page 148.)

The juices that come out of the ribs after they are braised are going to turn into the sauce, which is going to reduce so the flavors become concentrated. With this in mind, don't season the ribs with salt before searing them. Otherwise the sauce could end up pretty salty.

Yield: 6 servings

INGREDIENTS:

3 tablespoons vegetable oil
3 pounds boneless beef short ribs
2 cups sliced onions
8 cloves minced garlic
1 cup orange juice
1 tablespoon minced canned chipotle pepper
1 tablespoon dried oregano
salt and pepper

Heat oven to 325 degrees. Heat vegetable oil in a Dutch oven over high flame. Sear ribs on each side until there is some good color on them, about 3-4 minutes per side. Reduce heat to medium-low, add the onion and garlic, and sauté for several more minutes, stirring once or twice. Add the orange, chipotle and oregano. Cover and bake 1 1/4 to 1 1/2 hours. The time might differ depending on the size of the ribs. You want them to be tender, but not completely falling apart.

When ribs are done, remove them from the pan and cover with foil to keep warm. You can also at this point turn the oven off and place the covered ribs in there to keep warm.

Strain the mixture in the Dutch oven through a sieve into a bowl. Set aside the solids and let the liquid in the bowl settle for several minutes. There will most likely be a layer of fat on top of the liquid. To remove that fat, take some pieces of paper towel and gently lay them, and then remove them, one at a time on top of the liquid. This will remove most of the fat.

Place liquid back into the Dutch oven and boil over medium heat until reduced and slightly thickened. Add salt and pepper to taste. Add the onions back to the liquid and pour over the ribs. Dig in!!

Yield: 6 servings

GREEN CHILE CHICKEN ENCHILADAS

I love the fact that boneless and skinless chicken thighs are readily available in most grocery stores. They really make this dish moist, as opposed to breast meat, which can be dry.

The green chiles used here are usually found in 4- or 5-ounce cans. As for the poblano, you can read all about roasting peppers in the Poblano Cream Sauce recipe on page 80.

FILLING INGREDIENTS:

2 tablespoons vegetable oil
1 1/2 cups sliced onions
3 cloves garlic, minced
1 1/4 pounds boneless, skinless chicken thighs
2 cans (each about 4 ounces) diced green chiles
1 poblano pepper, roasted, peeled, seeded and chopped
1/2 cup tomato juice
2 teaspoons ground cumin
1 teaspoon chili powder
salt

OTHER INGREDIENTS:

8 eight-inch flour or corn tortillas
double batch of Tomatillo Salsa on page 83 (use the puréed style,
    not the chunky)
1 eight-ounce wheel of queso fresco
    (a fresh-style Mexican cheese), crumbled

To make the filling: Heat oil in a heavy sauce pan over medium flame, add onions and garlic and sauté them for several minutes. Add chicken and sauté for a few more minutes. Add green chiles, poblano, tomato juice, cumin and chili powder. Cover the pan and simmer over low heat until the chicken is cooked through and is just starting to fall apart, 15-20 minutes. Uncover and continue cooking to evaporate some of the liquid. At this point you want to pull the chicken apart with a fork so it's shredded and not in such big pieces. Add salt to taste. Set the filling aside until it's cool enough to handle.

To fill and bake the enchiladas: Heat oven to 350 degrees. Place equal amounts of filling into the tortillas, roll them up and place them into a lightly oiled 9-by-13-inch baking dish. Pour the tomatillo salsa over the top. Bake 20 minutes. Sprinkle the queso fresco on top and bake another 5 minutes.

Yield: 8 enchiladas

Mustard Fried Catfish

This is a recipe that I learned from a co-worker long ago and adapted with my own little twist. It just says "Southern cookin'."

In the teaching of my classes I've met people who say they don't care for catfish. The first thing I ask them is if they ate catfish that their dad or brother used to catch. They usually say yes, and that it tasted like mud. Well, these days almost if not all catfish is farm-raised and will not taste at all like wild-caught.

The "fried" in the title isn't necessarily true. The process is more like sautéing initially, and then finishing the fish in the oven. The reason I do this is the simple fact that I don't have a deep fryer in my kitchen. Also with this method the fish doesn't get too greasy.

Ingredients:

3 eggs
3/4 cup milk
1/3 cup plain old yellow mustard
1 teaspoon Tabasco red pepper sauce
6 catfish filets (7-9 ounces each)
2 cups coarse cornmeal
1 cup bread crumbs
    (Japanese-style panko crumbs work really well here)
1 tablespoon kosher salt
1 teaspoon black pepper
1/2 teaspoon garlic powder
1 teaspoon paprika
2 teaspoons dried thyme
1/2 teaspoon cayenne
oil for frying (peanut or vegetable)

To make the "eggwash," whisk eggs, milk, mustard and Tabasco in a bowl. Place catfish in the wash and set aside while you make the breading.

For the breading, mix all remaining ingredients (except the oil) in a baking pan, such as a 9 by 13-inch pan (this works better than a bowl).

The rule for breading things is, "One hand wet, one hand dry," meaning use one hand to dip the food in the eggwash and the other for the bread crumbs. This will insure that you don't bread your hands. If you are right-handed, place the fish to the right and the breading to the left. Now pick up one filet at a time with your right hand and let a little of the eggwash drip off of it. Lay the fish in the breading and give the pan a shake with your left hand. This will move some of the breading on top of the fish. Press the breading firmly into the fish and turn the filet over. Put some breading on top and press it in again. Place them in a single layer on a cookie sheet or platter. Repeat this until all the fillets are breaded.

Time to fry. Heat the oil to a depth of about 1/4 inch in a large sauté pan over medium high heat. Making sure not to crowd them, lay the filets flat side up in the oil and fry for about 20 to 30 seconds on each side. The breading should sizzle pretty well. This will just set the breading without cooking the fish too much. As you fry them, place the fillets on a flat baking sheet with shallow sides.* At this point, they can be held in the refrigerator for up to several hours.

To finish cooking the fillets, bake them in a preheated 400-degree oven 12 to 15 minutes.

*Some of the oil will come out of the breading when you bake it. The sides on the pan will prevent it from dripping onto the bottom of your oven. This will also prevent your spouse from having to remove the damn battery from the damn smoke detector.

Yield: 6 servings

SWEET CORN, PORK AND GREEN CHILE STEW

This has got winter comfort food written all over it. I love to make a batch of this or a big pot of chili for a crisp football Sunday.

A few notes on some of the ingredients: First, homemade Chicken Stock (see page 90) will give you the best flavor; although store-bought will work, too. Second, chicken can easily be substituted for the pork. Third, if you want to be a little more authentic, ditch the canned chiles and roast your own poblanos or whatever kind of chile you like.* One more thing: Feel free to use frozen or canned corn if you want.

INGREDIENTS:

2 tablespoons oil
1 1/4 pounds diced pork shoulder
1 1/2 cups diced red pepper
1 cup diced onion
3 cloves garlic, minced
kernels from 3 ears of sweet corn
1 cup canned green chiles
1 1/2 teaspoons ground cumin
1 teaspoon ground coriander
2 cups chicken stock
salt and pepper

Heat oil in a heavy stock pot over medium high heat. Add pork and sauté until just about cooked through. Feel free to get some good color on the meat. This will add to the flavor of the stew.

Add red pepper, onion, garlic, and corn. Sauté for several more minutes. Now add the chiles, cumin, coriander, and stock. Bring to a boil and turn down to a simmer. Simmer until pork is tender, 30 to 40 minutes. Add salt and pepper to taste.

* There are a couple methods for roasting chile peppers. The first is for a gas stove: Lightly coat the pepper in oil and place directly on one of the burners. Turn burner to high and roast pepper, turning it occasionally with tongs, until all the skin is black. Make sure not to get any of the skin gray; this means you have roasted it too much. The second method is for an electric stove (can you say eBay?): Coat peppers in oil and cut them in half. Lay them on a roasting pan and place under a hot broiler until the skins are black.

After either one of these methods, place the peppers in a sealed container or a sealed plastic bag. Let the peppers cool completely. Now just remove the charred skin and the seeds and veins from the inside of the pepper and you are ready to rock.

Yield: 6 to 8 servings

Tortilla and Pecan Crusted Mahi Mahi

I like to use blue corn tortilla chips in this recipe instead of yellow or white – the reason being that just in case you get a little color on the crust (some call it burning), the blue chips don't show the "color." To measure the chips, first crush them into smaller pieces with your hands and then measure them. And when grinding the pecans make sure not to go too far. The oil can start to come out and they will get really mushy.

Feel free to use whatever type of fish you like here. I go for the mahi mahi just as a personal preference; I like the firm texture and the fact that it's not a very oily fish (that way you won't get a lot of oil soaking into the crust). The crusted fillets work really well with a simple Butter Sauce (see page 66). I sometimes serve them with basmati rice, pan-seared spinach and tequila lime butter sauce.

Ingredients:

1 1/3 cups crushed blue corn tortilla chips
1 cup pecan pieces
1 teaspoon ground cumin
2 teaspoons pure olive oil
1 egg
6 six-ounce portions mahi mahi fillet
Butter Sauce, optional

Heat oven to 400 degrees. Grind the chips and pecans in a food processor separately. You want to get them to the consistency of coarse kosher salt. Place the chips and pecans in a bowl, add the cumin and olive oil, and mix well. You most likely won't need any salt because the chips were probably already salted.

Whisk the egg in a separate bowl. This is going to be the glue that holds the crust to the fish. Place the fillets on a greased baking pan. Make sure they are evenly spaced apart. Brush or spoon a light coating of egg onto each filet. Now take some of the crust and spread it on top of each filet to a thickness of about 1/4 inch. (If you have any crust left over you can keep it in the freezer for future use.)

Bake 17 to 20 minutes – the time will depend on the thickness of the fillets, which can vary. Serve with a butter sauce, if you like

Yield: 6 servings

Salmon and White Beans

This is a really simple dish that you can assemble ahead of time and throw in the oven when you're ready. It would also work well with chicken or with other fish such as halibut, cod or grouper. If you choose another fish you might have to change the cooking time because that will depend on the thickness of the fillets.

A few notes: The beans called for here can either be canned or you can soak and cook dried ones. (Use the canned if you are short on time.) To make the roasted garlic, see the recipe on page 113. As for the fresh herbs, I like the combination of parsley, thyme and rosemary with this dish; however whatever fresh herbs you might have available will probably work.

Ingredients:

2 tablespoons vegetable oil
1 1/2 cups diced onion
1 1/2 cups diced carrot
3 cups cooked white beans
1/2 cup roasted garlic
1/4 cup chopped fresh parsley, divided
2 tablespoons chopped fresh thyme, divided
1 tablespoon chopped fresh rosemary, divided
6 pieces (each 5 ounces) boneless, skinless salmon fillet
1 cup dry white wine
salt and pepper

Heat a sauté pan over medium flame. Add oil and swirl the pan to coat the bottom. Add onion and carrot and sauté for several minutes, until just cooked through. Mix the cooked veggies with white beans, roasted garlic and half of the herbs. Place bean mixture in the bottom of a 9-by-13 baking dish. Place salmon filets on top of bean mixture, spacing them evenly apart. Sprinkle the remaining herbs on top and add salt and pepper.

To bake: Heat oven to 350 degrees. Cover with foil and bake until the salmon is cooked through, about 20-25 minutes.

Yield: 6 servings

Salmon Hash

It may not be corned beef hash, but it's really good stuff. The fennel gives the dish a unique flavor that works particularly well with the salmon. It makes a nice meal with seared spinach, plus some aioli and fresh lemon wedges to accent everything.

A large skillet or nonstick pan is crucial here, in order to achieve nice, crisp potatoes. Also, the potatoes must be precooked before you sauté them in the hash. The best way to precook them is to dice them when they are raw and then simmer them in water until just cooked through, but still firm. Then drain well and completely chill the potatoes before sautéing them.

Ingredients:

2 tablespoons olive oil
1 1/4 pounds fresh salmon fillet, cut into 1 inch pieces
5 small red potatoes, diced and cooked as directed above
1 medium onion, diced
1 medium fennel bulb, quartered and sliced
1 large red bell pepper, seeded and diced
2 cloves of garlic, minced
3/4 cup lightly packed fresh basil leaves (about 1 ounce), chopped
salt and pepper

Heat oil in a large nonstick skillet over medium flame. Add the salmon, potatoes, vegetables and garlic (wait on the basil). Sauté until salmon is just cooked through and the veggies and salmon have a little color on them. You may need to turn up the heat so you aren't just steaming the ingredients. Make sure you either stir or toss often to cook everything evenly.

When salmon is just about cooked stir in basil and add salt and pepper to taste. Serve immediately.

Yield: 4-5 entrée-sized servings

SOUTHWEST SEAFOOD STEW

Close your eyes and imagine being near the beach in Mexico at a little outdoor café. The fresh fish market is within sight and the bowl of stew in front of you is just brimming with today's catch. Now open your eyes and come back to reality. Drink a margarita to help ease the pain, if necessary.

A (real) scene like the above was the actual inspiration for this dish. I was there, and it was so wonderful that I had to try to recreate it. I couldn't cook up the beach or the cafe, but I could manage the stew, and it turned out great.

This is a dish you can make ahead of time, at least part of it. Prepare the broth the day before or on the morning you plan to serve it, and then just add and simmer the seafood at meal time. The fresh cilantro at the end gives it a really nice touch. Another great thing about it is that you can add any type of seafood you want. If you want to plunk a whole lobster tail in, go for it! You can also give it a little more heat, if you like – add more of the poblano or some of your favorite hot sauce.

INGREDIENTS:

3 tablespoons olive oil
4 medium tomatillos (about 1/2 pound total), husked and chopped
3/4 cup chopped poblano pepper (or more to taste)
1 cup chopped onion
1/2 cup chopped tomato
4 cloves garlic, chopped
3 cups Shrimp Stock (see page 103) or bottled clam juice
juice of 2 limes
1 teaspoon cumin

seafood (use any or all of the following):
1/2 pound fresh fish chunks (mahi mahi, swordfish, whatever)
1/2 pound sliced calamari tubes
12 medium shrimp, peeled and deveined
12 medium scallops
1 pound fresh mussels
6 stone crab claws
salt
1/2 cup fresh cilantro leaves

Heat oil in a heavy stock pot over medium flame. Add and sauté the tomatillos, poblano, onion, tomato and garlic until they start to get soft. Make sure not to get too much color on the veggies. Add stock, lime juice and cumin. Simmer the mixture until all the veggies are soft, 20-30 minutes. Purée until smooth. At this point you can cool it off and chill it until meal time.

To finish the stew: If you have chilled the stew, bring it back to a simmer. Add the seafood and simmer until seafood is barely cooked, about 7 to 10 minutes depending on the size of your fish chunks. Taste and add salt, if needed. Divide stew into serving bowls, top with fresh cilantro and return to sweet Mexico.

Yield: 6 servings

Spice-Rubbed Pork Tenderloin

This is definitely a Dining Room fan favorite. Serve this with the Maple Bourbon Mustard Sauce on page 92. It also is fantastic with the Caramelized Onion and Bacon Relish on page 110.

The multi-spice mixture works really well with the pork. However you don't actually rub the pork with the spices, it's more like rolling it in them. Although rubbed sounds sexier.

The smoked paprika used here has become pretty mainstream and can be found in most grocery stores. Some companies even make a hot smoked paprika if you want to spice it up even more.

Coating the tenderloin with the spice mixture right before roasting is the key. This way the spices don't have time to get soggy, and you'll have more of a crust.

Any leftover spice mixture can be kept in the freezer for future use. It also works well with chicken or pork ribs on the grill.

Ingredients for spice rub:

1/4 cup chili powder
1/4 cup smoked paprika
2 tablespoons dried thyme
2 tablespoons dried oregano
1 teaspoon garlic powder
1 tablespoon kosher salt
1 teaspoon black pepper

Also:
2 to 2 1/2 pounds pork tenderloin

To make the spice rub, combine all ingredients. Also, heat the oven to 400 degrees.

To prepare the pork tenderloin, the first thing you need to do is clean it. This doesn't mean to wash it, but rather to remove the silver skin, which is the thin, tough whitish (or silvery) membrane that runs along parts of tenderloin and some other cuts of meat. (Believe me, you don't want to try and chew this stuff, unless you like pork-flavored bubble gum.) Slip the tip of a sharp boning knife just between the meat and the skin. Wiggle the knife back and forth until it comes out on the other side of the silver skin. Now gently cut under the silver skin until the knife comes to the end of it. Make sure to cut away from yourself! Repeat this until all the silver skin is removed.

Place the spice rub in a 9-by-13-inch pan or something similar in size. Place the pork on top of the spice rub and roll it around until well coated. Firmly press the spice rub into the pork with your hands so the spices create as thick of a coating as possible. (Your hands also will get spice-rubbed with this process. Latex gloves can prevent that, or maybe you just like getting a little messy.)

Place pork on a lightly greased baking sheet and roast for about 25 minutes. You want to reach an internal temperature of about 130 to 140 degrees; use an instant thermometer for this. Let the meat stand for about 5 minutes, then cut it on an angle into slices that are about 1/4-inch thick.

Yield: 6 servings

Green Thai Curry Shrimp

Some of the Thai-influenced recipes in this book call for store-bought curry paste. I like the purchased stuff mostly because it's convenient, and for the most part it has good flavor. But if you're ready for the real deal, then it's time to make your own. Think of it as a learning experience.

First we'll go through the special ingredients. You might not be familiar with a few of them, but they should be available in most Asian markets. Lemongrass is a lot like what it sounds – a lemony-tasting plant that looks like long, thick grass. Just make sure not to use any of the really fibrous out side layers. Galanga root is similar to ginger, but a little spicier and more fragrant. With that in mind you can substitute ginger root if you want. Thai chilies (which are usually labeled just that) are small, skinny and green or red. Shrimp paste comes in small plastic containers and is really stinky, but adds nice authentic flavor. And lastly the kafir lime leaves. They are sometimes found frozen as well as fresh. They add great fragrant citrus flavor.

With all that said, let's get cookin'! (And when the cookin' is done, serve your from-scratch shrimp curry over basmati rice as an entrée, or in smaller portions as an appetizer.)

Ingredients:

1/2 cup chopped lemongrass (tender inner shoots only)
2 tablespoons peeled and chopped galanga root
1 teaspoon ground cumin
packed 1/4 cup whole cilantro leaves
8 cloves garlic
10 Thai chilies, stems and most of the seeds removed*
1 teaspoon shrimp paste
2 kafir lime leaves
1/2 cup peanut oil
2 cans (each 13 ounces) coconut milk
2 teaspoons soy sauce
1 tablespoon cornstarch or arrowroot
2 tablespoons vegetable oil
2 pounds peeled and deveined medium shrimp

Place first nine ingredients in a food processor and purée until smooth. Put 2/3 cup of the purée in a heavy saucepan along with the coconut milk and soy sauce. Bring to a boil over high heat and reduce to low. Simmer for 5 to 10 minutes. Dissolve the arrowroot in a few tablespoons of water and whisk this into the sauce. Turn the sauce up to high just long enough for it to boil and slightly thicken. Set the sauce aside.

Heat vegetable oil in a short, large diameter stock pot over high flame. Add shrimp and sauté, stirring constantly, until center of shrimps are barely translucent, about 5-7 minutes. Pour sauce over shrimp and simmer over low for just a few more minutes until shrimp are done.

Yield: 6 entrée-sized or 12 appetizer-sized servings

* This might seem like a lot of hot chilies, but all the other ingredients help to calm it down a bit. Not all the way, but a bit. Also any leftover curry paste will keep for a week or two in the fridge. You could also freeze it, but it might not look as pretty when thawed.

ROASTED VEGETABLE TACO FILLING

If you have been to the restaurant, you know the type and style of cuisine we prepare. You probably wouldn't think that we would ever have tacos on the menu. And that's what my sous chef Jimmy thought, too. He bet me $50 that I would never have tacos on our menu. He was thinking of the traditional style of tacos, of course. And then I came up with the idea for a vegetarian taco. I won the bet but never made him pay. Call it a creative learning experience (for both of us).

Getting a little color on the vegetables adds a level of roasted goodness. You especially want to get a little color on the onions and the peppers, to help to bring out the sweetness in them. Roasting the veggies also evaporates quite a bit of moisture, which concentrates the flavor and keeps them from being too messy when eating. The only drawback to this cooking method is for the unlucky person who has to do the dishes. Roasting can leave a little bit of caramelized (some call it burned) veggies on the pan.

The sweetness of the orange juice and the smokiness of the chipotle called for here are a great combination with the roasted veggies. Top the tacos with the Creamy Avocado Sauce on page 62 and you have a vegetarian delight.

INGREDIENTS:

3 cups zucchini cut into 3-inch-by-1/2-inch sticks
3 cups portobella mushroom caps cut into 1/2-inch-wide slices
2 medium-sized red onions, cut into 1/2-inch slices
3 cups red bell peppers cut into 1/2-inch slices
3/4 cup orange juice
1/4 cup pure olive oil
2 tablespoons chopped fresh oregano
1 tablespoon chopped canned chipotle pepper
salt to taste

Heat oven to 400 degrees. Mix all the ingredients together in a large bowl. I like to use my hands for this so everything gets coated really well. Pour the vegetables onto an oiled 12-by-18-inch baking sheet and roast for 45 minutes to an hour. You might want to give them a quick stir about half way through.

Yield: enough filling for 6 to 10 tacos, depending on the size of the tortillas

Salmon Niçoise

I really enjoy the salmon in this easy-to-make baked dish. I think it is complimented well by all the different flavors going on. The sweetness of the fennel, the saltiness of the olives and capers, and the spunk of the herbs combine to make a super-tasty dish. And no heavy sauce, just a nice light broth.

It can be made two ways: You can put it all together in one large baking dish or in individual casseroles. Add some boiled potatoes on the side and bring out a nice bottle of wine, and you're all set.

Ingredients:

2 tablespoons olive oil
3 cups sliced fennel bulb
6 cloves garlic, minced
6 pieces (each six ounces) salmon
1 1/2 cups chicken broth or fish stock
    (bottled clam juice also works well)
finely grated zest and juice of 1 lemon
1/2 cup pitted Niçoise or Kalamata olives
3 tablespoons capers
1/4 cup chopped fresh parsley
1/4 cup chopped fresh basil
18 grape or cherry tomatoes, halved
salt and pepper

Heat oven to 400 degrees. Heat oil in a large sauté pan over medium flame. Add the fennel and garlic and sauté until fennel starts to wilt at the tips, about 5-7 minutes.

Place half of the fennel-garlic mixture in a 9-by-13-inch baking dish. Lay salmon pieces on top, spacing them evenly apart. Pour broth over the top of the salmon. Place the remaining fennel and garlic on the salmon. Arrange remaining ingredients on and around the salmon. Tent a piece of foil over the top of the pan, leaving space between the foil and the edge of the pan on either side. Bake until salmon is just cooked through, about 25-30 minutes.

Yield: 6 servings

camo night in the kitchen

it's a jungle in there..

It seems like there's always something creative happening in our kitchen – whether it's menu planning, wishing for a flat-screen TV in the kitchen (that didn't happen), or figuring out what kind of junk food we should eat that night.

Case in point: A few years back the kitchen staff was getting an order together for some chef pants. I think it was Jimmy who suggested we all buy a pair of camouflage pants and make Saturday night "Camo Night." Now every Saturday everyone working in the kitchen wears some type of camouflage clothing. (We decided not to go with the face paint.)

As the boss, I like to look at Camo Night as a team-building exercise or a bonding of the kitchen crew. I'm pretty sure the other guys in the kitchen just think it's cool.

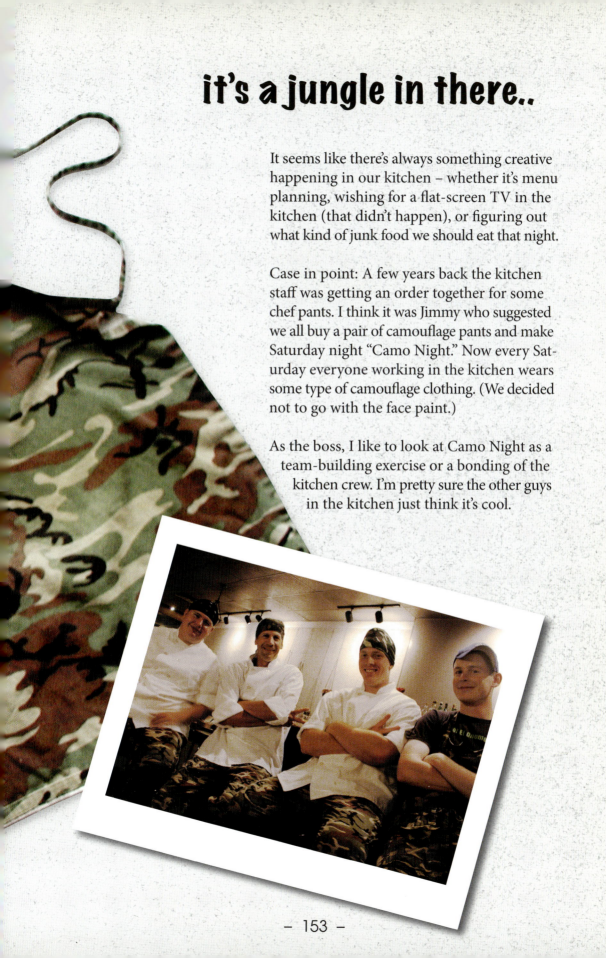

Desserts

Some of the desserts in this chapter are mainstays on the menu, while others have rotated onto the menu through the years. They're pretty simple and straightforward, but also delicious, and they will wow your friends and family.

I've never considered myself much of a baker, but it turns out that our Sticky Toffee Pudding (p. 168) has become our signature dessert, if not signature menu item. To tell the truth I rarely even make this dessert. I leave that to my capable staff. I suggest you make more than you think you need. They'll disappear, trust me.

desserts

Cardamom Custard Sauce

This is your basic crème anglaise dessert sauce, but with a little different flavoring. A classic crème anglaise is traditionally flavored with vanilla, but this has cardamom in it instead. Cardamom is a member of the ginger family and is available in most stores. It has kind of a sweet and spicy flavor.

This sauce is served cold, and is wonderful with pound cake, chocolate cake, cupcakes or just by the spoonful.

Ingredients:

4 egg yolks
3 tablespoons sugar
1 1/2 cups half & half
1 teaspoon ground cardamom

Bring a pot of water (just a couple inches worth) to a simmer. Meanwhile, whisk yolks and sugar together in a stainless steel or glass bowl. Place half & half and cardamom in a heavy sauce pan. Place over high heat and bring just to a boil, then remove pan from the heat right away. Slowly whisk half & half mixture into yolk mixture until well combined.

Place bowl containing the mixture over the pot of simmering water, (to create a double boiler). Whisk constantly until the mixture thickens and coats the back of a spoon. Strain through a sieve and chill immediately. The best way to chill it fast is to place the sauce (in its bowl) in a larger bowl that contains ice. Stir the sauce occasionally until it is chilled. This should take only a few minutes. (If you put the sauce in a plastic container when it's still hot it might overcook and curdle).

Yield: 1 3/4 to 2 cups

CHOCOLATE CAYENNE PATÉ

Cayenne, you say? With chocolate? Heck yeah! The sweetness and richness of the chocolate and cream start the taste sensation and are followed by a little heat from the cayenne. It's awesome.

I like to call this a pâté because of how it's served – like a slice of pâté, only one made of chocolate. It's actually chocolate ganache made into a loaf instead of used as a glaze. You could also just pour it into individual serving cups and then chill it. Either way works.

INGREDIENTS:

1 1/2 cups chocolate chips (just a little more than 1/2 pound)
3/4 cup heavy cream
1 egg yolk
1/4 teaspoon cayenne
fresh whole or puréed berries

Place the chocolate chips in a mixing bowl and set aside. Heat cream in a medium-sized sauce pan over high flame. When the cream boils, immediately pour it over the chips and whisk them until they're completely melted. Add the egg yolk and the cayenne and whisk until fully incorporated.

Lightly oil a 6-inch loaf pan and line it with plastic wrap. The oil will help keep the plastic in place. Make sure there is enough plastic to come up over the edges of the pan. Pour the chocolate mixture into the lined pan and refrigerate until firm – overnight is best, but 5 to 6 hours should do.

To serve, unmold the chocolate and peel the plastic off. Slice into 3/4- to 1-inch-thick pieces. Serve with fresh berries or a berry purée.

Yield: 6 to 8 servings

Chocolate Tart

This dessert has been a mainstay at The Dining Room since Day One. We serve it with a red raspberry purée, but any type of berries will work. It's super simple to make and quite elegant. It's basically a ganache, which is typically used to frost a cake. Here it's the entire dessert. It's chocolate. It'll work.

The cookies I like to use for the crust are the ones that start with an O and end with an O, but you can use any chocolate-type cookies you want. It's easiest to grind them in a food processor until they're the consistency of coarse sand. If you have any cookie crumbles left over, you can keep them in the freezer or just eat them.

For this recipe you'll need an 8-inch tart pan with a removable bottom and a fluted edge that's 1 inch high. Note that the recipe calls for a raw egg yolk, which enriches the tart. But if you're leery of using a raw yolk, it can be omitted.

Ingredients:

1 cup chocolate cookie crumbs
2 tablespoons melted butter
2 1/4 cups miniature chocolate chips
1 1/4 cups heavy cream
1 egg yolk (optional)

Mix crumbs and butter together and press into the side and bottom of the tart pan. It's easier to press the crumbs into the side first and then the bottom (rather than the other way around). It's also easier to use your hands – as opposed to a utensil – to press them in. Set the crust aside and get ready for the filling.

Place chocolate chips in a mixing bowl. Bring cream just to a boil in a deep, heavy sauce pan over high heat and immediately pour onto the chips. (The cream will rise quite a bit when it boils, so a deeper pan is recommended.) Whisk the cream and chips together until smooth. The heat from the cream will melt the chips. Now add the yolk and whisk until well combined. Pour the chocolate mixture into the crust and very gently spread the chocolate until it's evenly distributed.

Refrigerate the tart until set. This will take at least 3 hours.

Yield: 8 to 12 servings, depending on how hungry you are

Espresso Cinnamon Chocolate Ganache

Ganache is a wonderful thing. It's very versatile and can be flavored in many different ways—for instance, with some mint extract or Grand Marnier. It's basically heavy cream and chocolate that have been heated and mixed together. I like to add an egg yolk to give it a little more richness.

For this recipe we're going to flavor it with some cinnamon and instant espresso powder. If you can't find the espresso powder, instant coffee will work. You might need to add a little more as the espresso powder is stronger.

If you want you can serve this in espresso cups for a real fancy presentation.

Ingredients:

2 cups miniature semisweet chocolate chips
1 cup heavy cream
1/2 teaspoon cinnamon
1 tablespoon instant espresso powder
1 egg yolk
sweetened whipped cream (optional)

First thing to do is put your chocolate chips in a mixing bowl. (You're going be pouring hot cream over them and you need to do this as soon as the cream boils, so that the chips all melt.)

Combine cream, cinnamon and espresso powder in a heavy sauce pan over high flame. Bring it just to a boil. Pour it over the chocolate chips and whisk until the chips are completely melted. Add the yolk and whisk until well combined. Divide the mixture between 6 espresso cups or small dessert dishes. Chill completely before serving. Top them with some whipped cream if you want.

Yield: 6 servings

Red Wine Spiced Cherries

This is a really decadent dessert that can stand alone or be served with some unsweetened whipped cream. Presented in a tall martini glass it will be a show stopper. And how can you go wrong with cherries and red wine?

The cherries are the star in this recipe, and actually the frozen, pitted tart ones work the best. There are two ways that I find them in the grocery store. The first is in a bag and individually frozen so you can defrost any amount you want. The second, and the way I prefer, is frozen in their own juice. This way they are in one big frozen chunk, and you then get the juice for other uses (for instance, the Cherry Reduction Sauce on page 98).

Draining them well is the key here so the wine can make itself known. Best way to do that is to place them in a sieve for about ten to fifteen minutes. A two pound container of the cherries frozen in their own juice will yield about 2 1/2 cups of drained cherries. This might vary a bit on either side, but it will still end up being tasty.

Ingredients:

2 cups dry red wine (or you could start with 3 cups and just drink one
    to get it down to 2)
1/3 cup sugar
finely grated zest and juice of 1 orange
1/4 teaspoon allspice
1/4 teaspoon cardamom
3 cups thawed and well-drained pitted tart cherries

Bring wine and sugar to a boil in a small, heavy sauce pan and keep boiling it to reduce the liquid to about 1 1/3 cups. Remove from heat and add the zest, juice, allspice and cardamom. Place cherries in a stainless steel or glass bowl (don't use a plastic container because the container might get stained from the wine). Pour the wine mixture over the cherries. Refrigerate overnight (or just chill them thoroughly) and then enjoy. These will keep for up to a week, if not more. That is, unless, you eat them in the first day.

Yield: 6 servings

Orange Cinnamon Pound Cake

Through the years at the restaurant I've had several different pound cakes on the menu. I think this is my favorite. It is especially delicious with the Cardamom Custard Sauce on page 156.

The glaze that is used to "marinate" the cake overnight is key here. Once the cake is soaked in the glaze and completely chilled, it's best to slice it and heat it in a hot oven. This way the glaze will caramelize a little around the edges of each slice… but I'll get to that later.

The fact that it has to be completely chilled makes the recipe take a little longer than you might be used to. In other words, you need to make it at least a day ahead. Also, make sure not to over mix the batter. This will incorporate too much air and the cake might rise up out of the pan while baking and make a mess in your oven.

Cake ingredients:

2 1/4 cups sugar
1/2 pound unsalted butter, softened
1 teaspoon cinnamon
zest of 2 oranges, minced (save the orange flesh for the glaze)
1/2 teaspoon orange extract or orange oil
4 eggs
2 1/4 cups flour
3/4 cup half & half

Glaze ingredients:

1/3 cup sugar
juice of 2 oranges

Heat oven to 325 degrees. Spray a 12-by-5-inch loaf pan with cooking spray and lightly coat it with flour. Cream the sugar and butter in a table top mixer fitted with the paddle. Add the cinnamon, zest and extract and continue to mix on low. Scrape down the sides of the bowl as needed. (Sometimes it's easier to just remove the paddle and use that to scrape the sides.)

Add the eggs one at a time until well combined. Lastly add the flour and half & half at the same time. This might take a little coordination (not unlike rubbing your belly and patting your head at the same time). Mix until just combined, again scraping down the sides as needed. Pour batter into pan. Bake until a knife inserted in the center of the cake comes out clean – check this after 1 1/2 hours of baking time and then go a little longer if needed. Once the cake is done let it cool to room temperature. Now it's time for the glaze.

Combine sugar and juice in a small sauce pan and bring to a boil over medium heat. Turn heat down to low and cook until slightly thickened. This will take several minutes. Set aside until cool.

To glaze the cake, lay two sheets of plastic wrap next to each other, but over-lapping by a few inches. They should be at least 1 1/2 times as long as the cake. Unmold the cake and place in the middle of the plastic wrap top side up. Pour the glaze over the cake. (If it has cooled too much and is really thick, just reheat it slightly until it is thinner.) Now wrap the cake gently but securely in plastic, making sure to seal it really well. If you have any leaks just wrap a few more layers of plastic around it. Chill the cake in the refrigerator overnight.

To serve the cake, unwrap it from the plastic and slice into 1 to 1 1/2 inch slices. Place slices on a lightly oiled cookie sheet and heat in a preheated 425-degree oven 5 to 7 minutes. The side of each slice that was face down will get some good caramelization around the edges. That's the side you want to serve up so you can see all of the sugary goodness.

Yield: 8 to 10 servings

Lemon Curd

Think of lemon curd as a custard with citrus juice instead of cream or milk. It's used mostly as a filling between cake layers. I also like to serve it straight up with a few ladyfingers as a garnish or accompaniment.

In order to get a light texture to the curd, it's all in the wrist. The vigorous whisking action will incorporate more air into the curd, which will make it fluffier in texture. (I've never tried an electric whisk for this but I suppose it would work.) Note that you'll also need to cool down the curd as soon as it's done, so that it doesn't separate – which happens when the temperature stays too high for too long and the butter starts to pool on top. This can easily happen if it is put in a tightly covered plastic container when it is still hot.

The lemon in this recipe can be replaced with lime or orange, or a combination of any or all three. It can be made several days before you need it, if you think it will last that long in your refrigerator.

Ingredients:

1/2 cup fresh lemon juice
4 eggs
3/4 cup sugar
8 ounces (2 sticks) cubed, cold unsalted butter
finely grated zest of 1 lemon

Prepare an ice bath that will be used to chill the lemon curd right after it is cooked. Just fill a pan with ice or ice water and have it on hand.

Put some water in the bottom of a double boiler; bring it to a strong simmer on the stove. Place the lemon juice, eggs and sugar in the top part of the double boiler. Whisk the ingredients together until they're well combined. Place pan over the simmering water and keep whisking. The curd will start to thicken around the edges first, so scrape those with the side of your whisk as you go. Once the curd starts to thicken it will go pretty fast. When it is done it will coat the back of a spoon without running. Turn off the heat, but leave it on the stove top. Whisk in the butter a few cubes at a time until completely melted.

Next you want to cool down the curd immediately. Place the top of the boiler directly in the prepared ice bath. Now is also a good time to whisk the heck out of the custard to get it good and fluffy. Once it's cooled down, it can be served right away. Or cover and chill it thoroughly in the refrigerator – this will firm it up a little more.

Yield: 4 to 5 servings

Peanut Butter Caramel Sauce

Three simple ingredients, one tasty treat. This is a really nice little extra to have in the fridge for those special occasions, such as unexpected guests, midnight cravings or "Look! We have ice cream and it seems lonely."

The melting of the sugar might seem a little scary to some, but it's super easy. Just make sure you don't try to melt it too fast or it will burn before it all melts.

Ingredients:

1/2 cup sugar
1 cup heavy cream
1/3 cup peanut butter (smooth or chunky)

Place sugar in a heavy sauce pan and cook over medium low heat without stirring. You can swirl the pan now and then, but don't stir it. The sugar at first will start to kind of look like wet sand, and then will start to melt. Once it's all melted it will be golden brown in color. If it starts to smoke you've gone too far and will need to start over, because the sugar is burnt and not caramelized.

At this point you can remove the sugar from the burner, but make sure not to let it sit too long as the residual heat can keep it cooking and it could burn. Now add the cream and return it to the stove over medium heat. The sugar will mostly solidify once the cream hits it, but that's all right. Return the pan to the stove over medium heat and stir until the sugar has dissolved in the cream. Next, whisk in the peanut butter until well incorporated, and you're in business.

Yield: 1 3/4 cup

Peanut Butter Mousse

A spoonful of this in one hand and some chocolate in the other. Need I say more?

Ingredients:

1 teaspoon unflavored gelatin granules
1/4 cup cold water
1/4 cup sugar
1 3/4 cups heavy cream, divided
3/4 cup peanut butter (creamy or chunky – you choose)

Stir gelatin in the cold water in a small dish until dissolved and set aside. Place peanut butter in a medium bowl and set aside.

Bring sugar and 1/2 cup of the cream just to a boil in a small sauce pan. You just want the sugar to dissolve. Pour over peanut butter and whisk until well incorporated. Add gelatin mixture to the peanut butter mixture and mix well. Let cool until about room temperature. (Make sure not to let it cool too much or it won't combine well with the whipped cream.)

Whip the remaining cream until it holds medium-stiff peaks. Fold whipped cream into peanut butter mixture and refrigerate until set.

From here you can just scoop it into individual serving dishes, or just eat it right out of the bowl.

Yield: 5 to 6 servings

Sticky Toffee Pudding

Seven o'clock on a busy Saturday night at the restaurant and I get an overseas phone call. It's my stepfather, George, calling from London to tell me about this amazing dessert they have across the pond: sticky toffee pudding. After I calmed down from the fact that he called me on a Saturday night, I started some research. I found a few different recipes and played around with them a bit. I added some brandy to give it that Wisconsin feel.

It's a rich concoction, but if you look closely at the recipe you'll notice that a large portion of it is fruit. Can you say healthy dessert?

A few things to be aware of: When making the toffee sauce, don't leave it on the stove after it's done. Too much heat could cause it to separate, plus the sauce shouldn't be boiling hot when you serve it. As for the puddings, they will most likely fall a bit after baking, which will just make them more deliciously dense. They can be made several days ahead and warmed when ready to serve. To do this, warm them in a microwave oven on a low setting or in a 400-degree oven for 6 to 8 minutes.

Ingredients for the puddings:

6 ounces unsalted butter
1/2 cup lightly packed dark brown sugar
2 eggs
1 2/3 cups water
3 tablespoons brandy
6 ounces pitted dates*
scant 1 cup flour
2 teaspoons baking soda

Ingredients for the toffee sauce:

2 cups heavy cream
1/2 pound unsalted butter
1 cup dark brown sugar
1/4 cup dark corn syrup

Also:

toasted pecans (optional)

To make the puddings: Heat oven to 400 degrees. Butter (or oil or use pan spray) and flour 6 glass custard cups. Cream butter and sugar together with electric mixer until smooth. Add eggs and mix until well incorporated. Combine water, brandy and dates in a small saucepan; bring to a boil and then turn off the heat. Purée the date mixture in a blender. Be careful as this is very hot.

Combine flour and baking soda in a bowl. With the electric mixer running, add half the date mixture and half the flour mixture to the egg and butter mixture. Scrape down the sides of the bowl and add remaining halves of the two mixtures. Divide batter between prepared cups and bake until they have risen quite a bit and have gotten a little dark around the edges, 25-30 minutes. Let them cool to a warm temperature and then unmold them onto serving plates.

To make the sauce: Bring all ingredients to a boil in a tall, heavy pot. The mixture will rise in the pot quite a bit. Boil for several minutes, until butter is melted.

Note: If you make this ahead of time make sure to chill it immediately after the boiling so it doesn't separate. The best way to do that is the put the pot of toffee sauce in an ice bath.

To serve: Ladle about 1/2 cup of toffee sauce over each pudding and top with toasted pecans, if desired.

Yield: 6 puddings

* Dates are usually sold in 12-ounce packages so use about half a package. As long as you are close to 6 ounces the recipe will work fine. You can always make a double batch if you are unsure. Also, make sure not to buy the chopped dates as they are coated with sugar.

"The World's Best Non-chocolate Dessert"

Colin

My favorite dessert is sticky toffee pudding! It is at the restaurant the dining room! The dessert has carmel sauce, and a little cake. It is so good! It is the best dessert! I rekanend it.

little cake

carmel sauce

- My birthday party
- A wedding experience
- My favorite dessert
- Being the youngest/middle/oldest/only child
- A different topic idea __My favorite dessert__

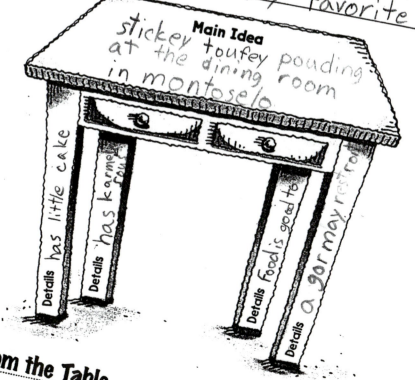

Main Idea
stickey toufey pouding at the dining room in montoselo

Details has little cake
Details has karmel sous
Details Food is good to
Details a gormay restron

ng from the Table

use the main idea and supporting

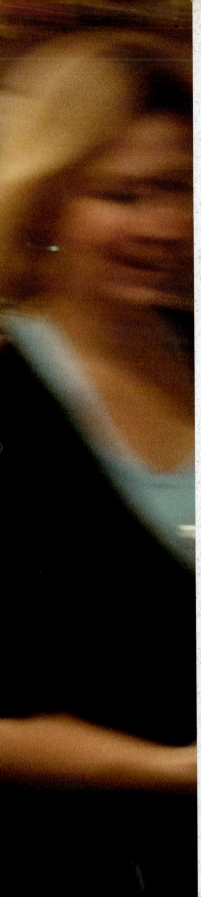

After a Busy Night

Restaurants have very different feel than many workplaces. On a busy night it's go, go, go in both the kitchen and on the floor, and throughout the hectic rush the staff has to perform a kind of choreographed dance to keep all the timing precise. Every plate of food has to come out fresh and hot and each course must arrive at the table at the right moment.

Then comes the end of the night: cleanup, paperwork, making lists to get ready for the next night, and so on. Usually after a demanding Saturday night I'll put out some food for the staff to eat while they are finishing up. And if a staff member has a birthday that week there's always a cake and a round of "Happy Birthday to You."

Another end-of-the-day task is the rehashing of how the night progressed. The kitchen staff will comment on how much or little a menu item sold, or maybe tell a story the part of the night we were "in the weeds." And of course, someone might give a gentle (or not- so-gentle) ribbing to a fellow co-worker for a harmless gaffe they made earlier in the evening.

The wait staff will talk about whether or not a lot of wine or cocktails were sold and who was in the dining room – longtime friends, regulars, first-timers or travelers who had just discovered us. Above all perhaps, this is a time for us to give ourselves a little pat on the back, or if need be, a little kick in the butt.

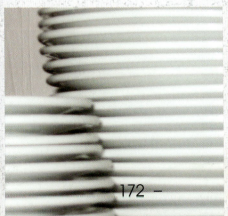

About the Author

Prior to opening his restaurant, The Dining Room at 209 Main, Wave Kasprzak had worked in restaurants for 15 years and had come up through the ranks of several Madison-area kitchens. He never had any formal training although he was fortunate to work alongside other classically-trained chefs. He did not want to work in a restaurant for the rest of his life because of the very long hours and because he had other interests. His mother-in-law Ruth convinced him to try opening a restaurant which would include the better side of restaurant life while still allowing time to "have a real life".

Fast forward 14 years… Wave has built an award winning destination restaurant which allows for him to pursue his interest in karate, golf in the summer, watch his beloved Green Bay Packers and spend holidays with family and friends. He will be the first to tell you that he did not do it alone… because it takes more than a chef!

Wave lives in Monticello, Wisconsin, just far enough away from the restaurant that the commute is short but still far enough not to be able to hear the phone ring after he leaves work. He lives with his wife and business partner Jane and his three royally pampered kitties.

Wave and Jane can be contacted through the restaurant website:
www.209main.com

Index

A

Appetizers 4-19

    Asian Tuna Ceviche 18

    Cornmeal and Five Spice Portobella Mushrooms 6

    Crawfish Cakes 8

    Fresh Herb Cheesecake 10

    Pepper Jack and Chèvre Queso Fundido 19

    Rare-Seared Truffled Beef Bruschetta 16

    Shrimp Cakes 12

    Tequila Lime Shrimp 14

B

BBQ Sauces

    Five Spice Raspberry 70

    Honey Bourbon 76

    Honey Habañero 77

Beef 17, 128-129

Broths

    Chicken 91

    Chipotle Shellfish 68

    Ginger Lemongrass Shellfish 69

C

Cheeses

    blue 64, 124-125

    Cheddar 22, 52, 54, 57

    chèvre 19

    cream cheese 11

    Gruyère 42, 43

    jack 47

    Parmesan 11, 37, 49, 52-53, 79

    pepper jack 19

    queso fresco 131

    cheese soup 22

Chicken 124-125, 130-131, 134, 138

Chocolate

    ganache 160

    pâté

    tart 158

Cream Sauces

    Blue Cheese 64

    Garlic 72

    Ginger Sherry 74

    Parmesan 79

    Roasted Poblano 80

D

Desserts 154-169

    Cardamom Custard Sauce 156

    Chocolate Cayenne Pâte 157

    Chocolate Tart 158

    Espresso Cinnamon Chocolate Ganache 160

    Lemon Curd 164

    Orange Cinnamon Pound Cake 162

    Peanut Butter Caramel Sauce 166

    Peanut Butter Mousse 167

    Red Wine Spiced Cherries 161

    Sticky Toffee Pudding 168

E

Entrées 122-151

    Blue Cheese and Walnut-Stuffed Chicken Breasts 124

    Chipotle-Braised Beef Short Ribs 128

    Cornmeal and Habañero Crusted Pork Cutlets 126

    Green Chile Chicken Enchiladas 130

    Green Thai Curry Shrimp 146

    Mustard Fried Catfish 132

    Roasted Vegetable Taco Filling 148

    Salmon and White Beans 138

    Salmon Hash 140

    Salmon Niçoise 151

    Southwest Seafood Stew 142

    Spice-Rubbed Pork Tenderloin 144

    Sweet Corn, Pork and Green Chile Stew 134

    Tortilla and Pecan Crusted Mahi Mahi 136

F

Fillings

    Roasted Vegetable Taco 148

Fish See Seafood

G

Go-Alongs 106-119

    Caramelized Onions 108

    Carmelized Onion and Bacon Relish 110

    Cranberry Chutney 111

    Ginger Chimichurri 114

    Honey Citrus Glaze 112

    Mint Chipotle Pesto 115

    Oven Roasted Tomatoes 116

    Roasted Pickled Garlic 113

    Roasted Tomato Gratin 117

    Two Olive Caper Relish 119

Grits 57

H

Hash, Salmon 140

Habañeros 77, 80, 126

Herbs 10, 37, 51, 66, 138, 151

M

Meat See Beef, Chicken, Pork,

P

Peanut Butter

    carmel sauce 166

    mousse 167

    peanut sauce 84

Peppers

    chipotle 23, 30-31, 65, 68, 128, 148

    green chile 135

    habañero 77

    jalapeño 14

    poblano 80, 130

    sweet red 26, 36, 66-67, 78, 148

Pork 126, 134, 144-145

Potatoes 46, 50-51, 54, 141

R

Reduction Sauces 89-103

    Apple Cider Brandy Reduction Sauce 101

    Cherry Reduction Sauce 98

    Chicken Stock 90

    Horseradish Cider Cream Sauce 100

    Maple Bourbon Mustard Sauce 92

    Port Peppercorn Reduction Sauce 93

    Red Wine Horseradish Reduction Sauce 94

    Red Wine Truffle Reduction Sauce 95

    Reduced Chicken Stock 90

    Roasted Tomato Reduction Sauce 96

    Shrimp Stock 103

    Vermouth Mustard Sauce 97

    White Wine Lemon Caper Reduction Sauce 99

Rice

    Arborio 43, 49

    basmati 48

    jalapeño 48

    risotto 42, 49

Roasted Tomatoes 65, 96, 116, 117

S

Salad Dressings 30-35

    Chipotle Caesar Dressing 30

    Ginger Miso Peanut Dressing 32

    Our House Salad Dressing 34

Salads 4, 36-38

    Chilled Salmon Salad with Indian Curry Vinaigrette 33

    Italian Bread Salad 36

    Poppy Seed Fennel Slaw 38

Salsas

    Mango Ginger Salsa 78

    Tomatillo Salsa 83

Sauces 60-87

    Black Bean Vinaigrette 63

    Blue Cheese Cream Sauce 64

    Butter Sauce 66

    Chilled Cumin Cream 71

    Chipotle Shellfish Broth 68

    Creamy Avocado Sauce 62

    Five Spice Raspberry Barbeque Sauce 70

    Garlic Cream Sauce 72

    Ginger Lemongrass Shellfish Broth 69

    Ginger Sherry Cream Sauce 74

    Honey Bourbon Barbeque Sauce 76

    Honey Habañero Barbeque Sauce 77

    Indian Curry Vinaigrette 87

    Mango Ginger Salsa 78

    Parmesan Cream Sauce 79

    Roasted Poblano Cream Sauce 80

    Roasted Tomato Chipotle Ketchup 65

    Smoked Tomato Remoulade 86

    Sweet Corn Sauce 82

    Thai Peanut Sauce 84

    Tomatillo Salsa 83

Seafood

    catfish 132

    mahi mahi 136

    salmon 33, 138, 140, 151

    shellfish 68

    shrimp 14, 146

Side Dishes 40-57

    Butternut Squash Risotto 42

    Cheddar Grits 57

    Chile Roasted Red Potatoes 46

    Creamy Parmesan Risotto 49

    Herb-Mashed Red Potatoes 51

    Jalapeño Rice 48

    Mashed Potatoes 50

    Parmesan Polenta 52

    Roasted Vegetable Caponata 44

    Sweet Corn Bread Pudding 47

    Zucchini Potato Pancakes 54

Soups 4, 22-27

    Beer and Cheese Soup 22

    Thai Curry Coconut Soup 25

    Three Mushroom Sherry Soup 24

    Tomato and Red Pepper Bisque 26

Squash

    Butternut 42

    Zucchini 45, 54-55, 148

Stocks

    Chicken Stock 90

    Reduced Chicken Stock 90

    Shrimp Stock 103

Stories

    About the Author 175

    After a Busy Night 172

    Camo Night in the Kitchen 152

    Cooking Classes 28

    How We Started 2

    Introduction 1

    Jane and Her Wine 120

    Mothers 20

    Our Kids 104

    Our Staff 58

    "The World's Best Non-chocolate Dessert" 170

T

Techniques

    breading 7

    butter sauce 14, 66

    cleaning mushrooms 6

    cooking garlic 72

    cooking shrimp 12

    cooking squash 42

    draining shredded vegetables 54

    handling jalapeños 14

    mixing cheesecake 10

    roasting corn 19

    roasting garlic 44, 72

    roasting vegetables 44

    sautéing 13

Truffles 16

This art installation is "**knit bombing**" which is covering an outdoor [item] with knitting. Cars, motorcycles, buildings, bus stops, trees, light posts retired NASA capsules and many other things nationwide are potential candidates to be "knit bombed". The squares in this install[ation] have been knit in the free form style taught by **Valentina Devine** of [Los] Alamos, New Mexico. Inside The Dining Room at 209 Main there is [a] display of Valentina's garments, all designed and knit and/or crochet[ed by] her - all one of a kind.

This installation commemorates the "new main street" and its celebra[tion] on October 23, 2010.

Contributors: Marilyn Christensen, Mary Ellen Rauch, Karen Scamme[l,] Ruth Sybers

Cooking Notes:

Cooking Notes:

Cooking Notes:

Cooking Notes: